PRAISE FOR *THE COLSON WAY*

"Owen Strachan has given us a compelling account of Chuck Colson's joyful and determined life of Christian witness and service. Those of us who knew him well and worked alongside him in promoting Christianity as a worldview, and not merely a religion of private piety, recognize him in the discursive portrait Strachan provides. The Colson Way is a praiseworthy intellectual achievement and a gift to the Christian community."

—Robert P. George, McCormick Professor
of Jurisprudence, Princeton University

"Chuck Colson was a valued mentor and trusted friend. He possessed a rare combination of hardheaded political smarts with a heart that had truly been transformed by Jesus. I regularly sought his guidance and counsel over the years, and never was found wanting. His courageous, winsome public witness and prophetic voice are sorely missed in the troubled times in which we live. This is precisely why *The Colson Way* needed to be written, and ought to be required reading for any Christian seeking to engage in the public square."

—Frank Wolf, Senior Distinguished Fellow,
21st Century Wilberforce Initiative

"I was privileged to know and work with Chuck Colson in several respects. He was a man of character and conviction who understood that believers find themselves in 'two cities,' as Augustine wrote. As a member of the city of God, I have dedicated my life to strengthening the city of man. I am so thankful to see Owen Strachan's *The Colson Way* celebrate this kind of vision. I commend it highly and urge pastors and churches to buy this book—and to share this vision with their people."

—Mike Huckabee, former Arkansas
governor and host of Fox TV's *Huckabee*,
and bestselling author of numerous books—
most recently *God, Guns, Grits, and Gravy*

"*The Colson Way* is an honest, enjoyable, and eye-opening look at one of the most significant Christian leaders of the twentieth century. Strachan not only captures the story of Chuck Colson, he offers invaluable insights along the way. I hope this book is widely read by Christians of all ages, but especially young Christians who will be both equipped and inspired by Colson's life."

—Sean McDowell, Ph.D., Professor at Biola
University, international speaker, and author
of *The Fate of the Apostles*

"A precious gift to the rising generation of evangelical leaders! In an era where cultural compromise is the trend, *The Colson Way* introduces a fearless advocate for the faith, family, and freedom, whose story of accountability and unwavering conviction is one every young Christian should know."

—Chelsen Vicari, author and Evangelical
Action Director at the Institute on Religion
and Democracy

"Owen Strachan has very capably applied his considerable intellect and writing skills to interpreting the life and accomplishments of one of the most important Evangelical leaders of the last half century. It's impossible to understand the recent history of Christianity in America without knowing Chuck Colson's story. God raised him up for special purposes, and Colson leaves no clear successor as a collator of ministry, activism, and intellectual life. Hopefully this book will help inspire future Chuck Colsons."

—Mark Tooley, President, Institute on
Religion and Democracy; author of *The
Peace That Almost Was*

"This book introduces Charles W. Colson to a new, younger generation that 'knew not Chuck.' In a time of retrenchment and retreat, the 'Colson way' calls us to fidelity, resolve, and hope. Chuck pursued this path with courage and love, and so must we."

—Timothy George, founding dean of
Beeson Divinity School of Samford
University, featured writer for *First Things*

"Owen Strachan's new biography of Chuck Colson is timely, engaging, and insightful. Even more important, it's needed. For a generation of evangelicals who came of age without many positive examples of cultural engagement, Strachan's profile of Colson is a challenging reminder that we can—and must—venture into the public square for the glory of God and the good of our neighbor. I believe Chuck would be deeply honored by this tribute to his legacy of faith and service."

—Jim Liske, President and CEO, Prison
Fellowship Ministries

"As someone who was for four years Charles Colson's first research assistant when he returned from prison, I thought I knew everything there was to know about Chuck. Not so. Strachan introduces present-day evangelicals (and others) to one of the most unique, and surprising, social reformers in the broader Christian world of the past fifty years. He communicates with a clear and engaging writing style and paints a moving portrait of a true American, Christian original. No wonder, when his whole life is seen in full, that he won warm admiration and respect from so many of his former critics. This vivid, lucid, and informative biography offers a ringing endorsement as to why this is so."

—Michael Cromartie, Vice President, Ethics
and Public Policy Center, Washington DC

"I'm often asked what it was like to work with Chuck Colson. I haven't yet figured out how to answer. All I know is that I am different because of him, and so are many, many others. In *The Colson Way*, Strachan artfully describes what I struggle to communicate about this great man. And, I am convinced that those who read this book, like this person who encountered Chuck's life, will be inspired to live culturally redemptive lives, loving God and people."

—John Stonestreet, Speaker and Fellow,
the Chuck Colson Center for Christian
Worldview; Senior Content Advisor,
Summit Ministries

"Congratulations are due to Owen Strachan for producing this highly readable and thoughtfully presented book on the life and work of Chuck Colson. This volume offers illuminating insights into the motivation and manner of 'the Colson way' as it developed from the early days of his post-conversion ministry to Colson's more mature role as evangelical statesman, leader, and mentor. Admirers of Colson will find their appreciation of Colson enriched, even as they are encouraged to extend Colson's culture-renewing vision to the next generation. Those unfamiliar with Colson's life and work will be challenged to follow Christ with renewed courage and faithfulness."

—David S. Dockery, President, Trinity
International University

"We live in a disillusioned culture hungering for authentic heroes. History will record that Chuck Colson was a prophetic voice and a truly transformational leader. As his pastor and close friend, I knew and loved him. Unlike a mountain which is majestic in the distance and craggy up close, the better I knew Chuck, the more I respected him. Owen Strachan's marvelously insightful book is a lively read that inspires us in the Colson Way. 'Overcome evil with good' (Romans 12:21). May a whole new generation be 'born again' and renew the 'good fight.'"

—Dr. Hayes Wicker, Senior Pastor, First
Baptist Church Naples (Chuck Colson's pastor)

"In this accessible biography of a spiritual giant, Owen Strachan has laid the foundation to retrieve the timelessness of Chuck Colson's public witness. What Strachan shows is that Chuck Colson put first things first—gospel first, public life second. It was never as though public life was less important. It was all where the accent rests; and as Strachan writes of Colson, the accent rests first upon gospel, and secondly, on its transforming effects on society. I can't calculate the degree to which Colson's heroism and legacy towers. But in the *The Colson Way*, Strachan explains the 'how' and the 'why' of one of America's most important religious and political figures."

—Andrew Walker, Director of Policy
Studies, The Ethics and Religious Liberty
Commission; author of *Marriage Is*

"Chuck Colson was one of the most important figures in American Evangelicalism in the last half of the 20th century. He was a complex man who was deeply concerned for the Christian worldview and at the same time participated in some of the most significant events and controversies of the Evangelical movement in the last several decades. But, more than anything else, Chuck Colson was a man who had come to know the Lord Jesus Christ as savior and his testimony of conversion to Christ—demonstrated through long decades of Christian leadership—is an important part of that story. Owen Strachan offers us invaluable insight into the life of Chuck Colson and the trajectory of 20th-century Evangelicalism."

—R. Albert Mohler, Jr., President, The
Southern Baptist Theological Seminary

"Chuck Colson was a profound inspiration for so many of us concerned with bringing the truths of the gospel to the public square and to the most pressing issues of the day. Owen Strachan has managed to write an accessible and gripping biography of Colson that also builds on Colson's agenda for cultural renewal, encourages the weary, and serves as a wake-up call for the thousands of faithful but timid Christians who are still wondering if they can make a difference. This book needed to be written, and Strachan was just the man to write it."

—Jay Richards, Ph.D., Assistant Research
Professor, Catholic University of America;
Executive Editor, *The Stream*

"Chuck Colson was a friend and a mentor to me—and I'm not the only one who can claim this. His influence continues to be felt not only inside the Church but in the culture at large. I'm thankful that Owen Strachan has taken the time to pay tribute to this unique and important hero of the faith."

—Jim Daly, President, Focus on the Family

"Owen Strachan is an essential voice for millennials. His message urges all of us to look beyond emotion for transcendent truth. Buy *The Colson Way* especially for the young person searching. They'll be engaged by a remarkable story and equipped for a life of bold faithfulness."

—Penny Young Nance, CEO and President,
Concerned Women for America

"*The Colson Way* introduces millennial Christians to a hero of the faith, who was committed to redeeming society, from prison cells to the halls of power. Through lessons and examples from Colson's life, Strachan winsomely provides guidance and encouragement to young Evangelicals on how we can be 'boots on the ground' for Christ, no matter what our calling, in a culture that desperately needs witnesses to the truth."

—Bethany Goodman, Assistant Director,
March for Life Education and Defense Fund

"Millennials are desperately seeking Christian role models whose lives are marked by authenticity, transparency, and fearlessness in pursuit of justice. Owen Strachan has done them a tremendous favor by introducing Chuck Colson. His incredible story—of a great fall followed by salvation and world-changing redemption—is an example to those wondering what faithfulness looks like in these tumultuous times."

—Eric Teetsel, Executive Director,
Manhattan Declaration

"Chuck Colson was larger than life. His life and career were the canvas upon which God wrought a masterpiece of grace. If Colson's life and times tell us anything, it's that the Lord's arm is not too short to save. Owen Strachan has given us a powerful portrait of the man and his work. It is a marvelous story of an imperfect man, and Strachan tells it in this riveting account. I am so thankful for this important book on one of evangelicalism's leading lights. It is a signpost for a new generation that needs to take their public witness as seriously as Colson did."

—Denny Burk, Professor of Biblical Studies,
Boyce College

"Years ago, my sleeping faith was awakened by Charles Colson's insights into the ways in which the Gospel governs all of reality. Now, in *The Colson Way*, Owen Strachan introduces Colson's life and work to a new generation—and reminds the rest of us that Colson's example of cultural engagement and public-square witness is as relevant and necessary as ever."

—Karen Swallow Prior, Ph.D., author of
Booked: Literature in the Soul of Me and
*Fierce Convictions—The Extraordinary Life
of Hannah More: Poet, Reformer, Abolitionist*

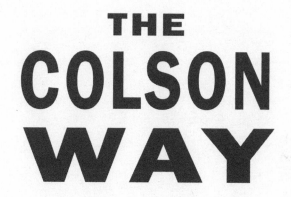

THE
COLSON
WAY

THE
COLSON
WAY

Loving Your Neighbor and Living with Faith in a Hostile World

OWEN STRACHAN

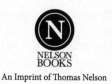

NELSON
BOOKS

An Imprint of Thomas Nelson

Published in Nashville, Tennessee, by Nelson Books, an imprint of Thomas Nelson. Nelson Books and Thomas Nelson are registered trademarks of HarperCollins Christian Publishing, Inc.

Published in association with the literary agency of Wolgemuth & Associates, Inc.

Thomas Nelson titles may be purchased in bulk for educational, business, fund-raising, or sales promotional use. For information, please e-mail SpecialMarkets@ThomasNelson.com.

Library of Congress Control Number: 2015931026

ISBN: 978-1-4002-0664-3

Printed in the United States of America

15 16 17 18 19 RRD 6 5 4 3 2 1

To Eric Metaxas, practitioner of the Colson way

CONTENTS

FOREWORD

by Eric Metaxas

When I came to faith in the summer of 1988, I was convinced that being a serious Christian—a *born-again Christian*, as I would then have put it, and still do—was so *outre* that no one who was anyone could be one. Billy Graham, who comprised his own category, was the exception. But other than him, the culture was wall-to-wall secularists. So when I discovered Chuck Colson of Watergate fame might be a born-again Christian, I flipped. If it turned out to be true, he would be my hero. Happily, it was, and he's been so ever since. But who was Chuck Colson?

I was in sixth grade when Watergate exploded across the national consciousness in 1973. Though it was impossible to follow the scandal's serpentine windings, everyone—from the paper boy to Johnny Carson—seemed to talk endlessly of strange things like "the tapes" and "the missing eighteen and a half minutes" and "Bebe Rebozo." Those who hated Nixon wanted him impeached, but his defenders said every president since FDR had secretly taped their Oval Office conversations, so what was the big deal? They thought he should thumb his nose at his enemies by burning the tapes on the White House lawn.

Then one hot August day the controversy ended. I was in a

motel room with my parents on the North Fork of Long Island and there on the TV set was Richard Milhous Nixon, resigning the presidency of the United States "effective at noon tomorrow." For an idealistic boy whose father admired Nixon, it was mind-blowing stuff. In truth, America would never be the same. To see high public officials held accountable for their crimes and sent to jail was breathtaking.

One of the President's Men, as they came to be called, was notoriously known as "the White House hatchet man," willing to do anything to help the president get reelected. This was Chuck Colson. As it turned out, Chuck would go to jail for his misplaced zeal, as so many of them would. But what makes Chuck's story far more interesting than the others is that before he went to jail he found Jesus, and after he got out of jail he determined to spend the rest of his life going back into jails, to help prisoners. In short, God had palpably changed Chuck Colson, and what might simply be a cautionary tale about a precipitous fall has become the story of a spectacular redemption.

So when I learned in 1988 that Colson was a born-again Christian, I was enormously inspired. Chuck was decidedly unlike the embarrassing televangelists who were then all over the newspapers, whose moral and sartorial failings brought ignominy to the faith. I bought his books, *Born Again* and *Loving God*, and devoured them both, not least because they helped me see it really was possible to be brilliant and profoundly serious about one's Christian faith. But Chuck's life showed me even more: that it was possible to live out one's faith. In 1976, he founded Prison Fellowship, and although he spoke to all kinds of groups around the world, he often preached in prisons and prayed with men on death row. As far as I was concerned, this was Johnny

Cash with an Ivy League degree and a Brooks Brothers suit. Here was someone worth emulating.

In 1993, Chuck began doing a daily radio commentary called *BreakPoint* and as I was driving around Fairfield County, Connecticut, I would listen. In them, Chuck did what no one else seemed to do: he connected his faith to the culture, to things like popular books and TV advertisements. I vividly recall his column in *Christianity Today* on Woody Allen's film *Crimes and Misdemeanors*. A born-again Christian who appreciated a Woody Allen film? Was that even permissible?

One day in 1995 I heard Chuck was speaking at the Yale Law School and I sped thither to meet him, handing him a typed fan letter. Since I knew he had a grandson, I gave him a copy of my *Uncle Mugsy* children's book too. A week later I was stunned to get a letter from Chuck, saying he would keep my name in his files in case our paths crossed again. I was further flummoxed when a year after that I heard from his office that they were looking for a new script writer/editor for *BreakPoint*. I leapt at the opportunity, and soon found myself working for the man himself. In the two years that I did so, seeing no daylight between his public and private personae, my respect for him only deepened.

But when our daughter was born in 1999, needing more money than a ministry could pay, I sadly bade Chuck and *BreakPoint* adieu and skipped off to write for Bob the Tomato and Larry the Cucumber—who never did time in a federal prison, that we know of. For some years thereafter I saw little of Chuck, again admiring him from a distance. But when in 2010 my *Bonhoeffer book* came out, our relationship was rekindled. Chuck was positively effusive about the book, talking about it everywhere he went. That the man I deeply revered thought so well of anything I had done was almost too much to bear. But it was because more than anyone, he saw the parallels between how religious liberty was destroyed in the Third Reich and how it was eroding in our own culture. As the man who put the *Manhattan Declaration* on the map, he knew religious liberty to be of paramount importance and so he spoke of it at every opportunity, as I am privileged now to do.

The last time I saw Chuck was when he spoke his last public words in the spring of 2012. I was just behind him when he was stricken, as you will read later in this book, and even then he spoke passionately about Bonhoeffer and religious freedom. But everyone who knew him felt it fitting he should go out with his boots on. He was a Marine. He was a Christian. He was the real thing.

In latter years I've been amazed that many younger Christians haven't heard about Chuck Colson. That needs remedying, and for my part, I made him one of the great men in my *SevenMen* book. But far better is the book that follows this foreword. Here is the full treatment that Chuck's life deserves, and one that will inspire a new generation of devotees to what its author has aptly dubbed "The Colson Way." That a young evangelical intellectual of Mr. Strachan's caliber has been drawn to this subject is a profound encouragement. Chuck's life should be known to anyone wanting the kind of faith that, in the end, is the only kind—one in which one's mind and actions are both robust, and inextricably intertwined.

Finally, the book's dedication—which I have only recently seen—so bowls me over I must refuse to think of it, unless I may see it as a wild typographical error that eluded the book's otherwise crackerjack editors. But this book that honors me so is indeed a gem, and a worthy introduction to one of the very greatest men of recent times. May God use it in your life, dear reader.

Eric Metaxas
New York City
March 2015

INTRODUCTION

It was an innocent trip. I was in pursuit of spaghetti, perhaps, or maybe an Italian sandwich. This was a part of my regular routine as a staff intern at the U.S. Department of State in Washington, DC. Every weekday morning I braved the Metro, hoofed it several blocks to the great stone rectangle that is the State Department building, and there commenced a struggle with the mailbox code lock. This is what DC interns did: they got the mail, unlocked the office, answered any early morning phone calls, and handled filing and photocopying. By midmorning I was usually ready for lunch.

The lowly position of staff intern at the State Department was nonetheless an exciting one for a boy from small-town Maine. Growing up, I was familiar with the city in the same terms as most Americans: from the nightly news video footage. Now, in 2004, I wasn't watching coverage of the halls of power—I was walking them. I worked for the White House at State in the Office of White House Liaison. It was a heady role: I escorted political appointees to various offices, faxed resumes to the Baghdad Palace in the midst of the Iraq War, and handled phone calls from a dizzying array of very important people. I was in close proximity to greatness but had not directly encountered it. Until, that is, I went hunting for some pasta.

As I rounded the corner in the vast but empty cafeteria of the State Department, I came face-to-face with Colin Powell himself: regal, ramrod straight, wearing his crisp jacket with row upon row of military decorations. I froze—just the Secretary of State and me.

"Hello," I said meekly.

"Hi," he said with a nod.

Colin Powell and me: two men united by an affinity for late-morning pasta.

———

My fleeting brush with global leadership multiplied several times over in America's capital. I walked past a bleary-eyed Ted Kennedy late one night on Capitol Hill, where I lived. I went to the White House for one of President George W. Bush's helicopter departures. When Ronald Reagan died, I stood in a very long line to see him lying in state. DC was, and is, a head-turning place. It may be the "nerd Hollywood," but you can barely exit an overcrowded Metro stop without bumping into a wonkish celebrity.

There is a metaphor here for Christians in the American public square. Evangelicals have entered the halls of power. In some cases, actually, we built them, only to be ushered out later. In other cases, we came late to the soiree. But though we find ourselves in the great societal conversations of the age, we often struggle to know exactly what to say. This is especially true of young evangelicals. We know we want to be a voice for life and liberty and happiness in our time, but we're not confident in our voice.

Millennial Christians—those born in the 1980s or later— do know very clearly what they *don't* want to be. As a child of

1981, I'm aware of our desire to avoid social awkwardness, for example. Few things are worse in the age of entertainment monoculture than this: being the weird one, the person who talks too loudly, shows exceeding earnestness, and voices opinions too rapidly. Beyond this, we want to be liked, to be popular, and to have lots of "friends" and "followers" on social media. When it comes to politics in particular, we want to be a voice of fairness.

Many young Christians, I sense, feel that they have few public-square role models. This is not true in every category. If you want to be a preacher, you've got numerous faithful figures—Mark Dever, John Piper, Tim Keller. If you want to be a Christian academic, there are many examples—Mark Noll, Al Mohler, Karen Swallow Prior. If you want to be a public intellectual or media personality, one thinks of Eric Metaxas, Shannon Bream, and Lauren Green. But to whom does one turn to find a modern public-square exemplar? This is a trickier matter. Many of us might point to Dietrich Bonhoeffer or Martin Luther King, Jr., but is there anyone in the last forty years who comes to mind?

I think there is. This book is forged in the conviction that there is at least one major public figure of recent vintage who serves as a faithful evangelical model for public-square witness and cultural engagement. This man is Charles Wendell "Chuck" Colson. Colson is known to many Christians but, lamentably, to far fewer millennials. He was born in 1931 and died in 2012, and enjoyed his heyday while many of this generation were in diapers. His voice was prominent during their youth, but my hunch is that for many millennials, Colson is not front and center on their cultural radar.

He should be. Chuck Colson was a brilliant, shrewd, winsome man, a courageous public-square leader who practiced an invigorating brand of cultural engagement. In terms that resonate with a generation attuned to authenticity, he was no square. He wore thick, dark glasses before they trended globally, searched relentlessly for ways to engage young people, and in his seventies experienced a certain thrill when he mastered the fine art of the iPad. Colson stayed young until he died, exhibiting a much younger man's energy for travel and hard work, thrilling to the challenge of a new project or speech, throwing himself into training emerging leaders in order to strengthen the public witness of the church.

On numerous issues, Colson spoke prophetically. Years after his political career ended, Colson had a fantastic ability to predict the trends and twists of American society. He used this rare ability to lead and, if necessary, retrofit the many operations he led, ensuring that his ministry was always a relevant one.

But Colson was not merely dynamic. He was courageous. This, perhaps, is what a generation thirsting for genuineness might find most attractive about Colson. Many millennials, after all, have witnessed upheaval. We have experienced heartbreak—divorce, infidelity on the part of our parents, moral failings by public figures both local and national, the slow, trickling loss of confidence in one scandal-plagued institution after another.

What many people desire today is quite simple: authenticity. We believe in the good. We want justice. We crave models. But we have a hard time believing that either individuals or institutions will embody virtuous ideals. In Chuck Colson, we find an example of an internationally known believer who fought the good fight and stayed faithful to the end.

I come to praise Colson, but not to lionize him. Many who are familiar with him, after all, have only heard about him because he was "Nixon's hatchet man," or because he was once reported to have said, "I would run over my own grandmother" for political purposes, or because he was embroiled in Watergate and went to prison for his involvement. To some, he is still a disgraced figure. The mainstream media has little love lost for Richard Nixon even today, and the same distaste is felt for those who worked closely with him. Some readers may have picked up this biography with a high degree of skepticism about Colson.

We will cover Colson's role in the corrupted Nixon White House and Watergate in coming chapters. I will offer no contorted apology for him. Before his conversion, he was by his own account a tough customer. His autobiography, *Born Again*, does not shy away from frank discussion of his proud and morally questionable behavior in his political career. Colson was a fallen human being. He was conscious of his flaws and sins and would not have wanted a whitewash of his life. He was a part of the Nixon White House, and though he did a fraction of what was alleged, he nonetheless performed deeds that were immoral. Sin was not just in the system but also in Colson himself.

This is not a book on Watergate, but we will cover that period and clarify Colson's role in the tumultuous and controversial days of Nixon's presidency. Just last year, America witnessed the fortieth anniversary of Nixon's resignation from presidential office. This anniversary brought a wave of new sources and books into the cultural conversation. Colson remains relevant for not only spiritual reasons but also political ones. For our purposes, another anniversary is still more relevant. The year 2015 marks the fortieth anniversary of his release from prison—or, as it might be called, the unleashing of Chuck Colson for ministry to the fallen and forgotten.

It is my hope that my efforts will allow an entire generation of young evangelicals to find great encouragement in their own witness for Christ in these conflicted times. This book is not a definitive biography of Colson, but it does add a good deal of material to the Colson corpus. Jonathan Aitken published an early attempt at such a work in 2005, *Charles W. Colson: A Life Redeemed*, furnishing us with an illuminating and thoroughly researched study of the man and his work.

I am thankful for the depth of Aitken's research and have profited from his lively and incisive portrait. That book had to leave off well before Colson's career and life ended, however. Alongside Eric Metaxas's chapter in *Seven Men*,[1] *The Colson Way* fills out the story. This full-length book, the first published since his death in 2012, reviews the last decade of his life (and his death), adds numerous unknown biographical details and touches, and includes the valuable testimony of many eminent interviewees, many of whom had not previously shared their insights. In sum, I present Colson in the mold that best fits the broad span of his life and work: his public-square witness.

This book seeks to accomplish two major aims: first, it tells the overall story of Colson's life with special reference to the motivation and accomplishments of his public-square work. Second, it forms this historical material into a compelling model for Christian public witness and cultural engagement. In the pages that follow, we do not only recount his work, but we apply it, considering how his witness shapes and informs our own. What was the Colson way? How may we learn from it, be encouraged by it, and even put it into practice? That is my burden in the pages that follow.

The idea for this book came after I gave the Family Policy

Lecture in 2012 at the Family Research Council. My address was called "The Sacrificial Witness of the Christian Moral Tradition." As I chewed on the themes from the talk and mourned Chuck Colson's death in late 2012, I recognized that Colson was not well known among my peers. I had read *Born Again* a decade earlier and was stirred by it. Many of my millennial friends have not read the book, however. Colson's incredible story needed to be told afresh.

This is no mere historical study. I want this book to wake up a generation. There are thousands of young believers who are struggling to find their voice in the contested American public square. These Christians love the Bible, trust its teaching, and ground their identities in the soul-saving cross of Jesus Christ. They sing Hillsong and LeCrae and Mumford and Sons in their cars, they capture epic life events on Instagram, they recoil when they think of tiny babies being aborted in the womb, they enjoy visiting big cities, and they are trying to figure out how to be meaningfully Christian in a world that more and more seems to find them deficient.

These young evangelicals aren't angry. They don't throw fireballs. They are my friends, neighbors, and students. I rub shoulders with them in my day-to-day work teaching theology and history to college and seminary students. And I want them to see that being a publicly minded Christian does not mean being old. It doesn't mean being white. We need to remix what it means to be a Christian in public. Biblical ethics born of the gospel and bearing on every aspect of life cross all boundaries and divides—racial, social, economic, educational, geographic.

Our unity is not ultimately grounded in a political program, important as that is. It is not grounded in anger or fear or despair.

It is grounded in Jesus Christ, crucified and ruling over all the world. It is Jesus and no other who would have us stop dividing ourselves needlessly and privatizing our public convictions. It is Jesus who beckons us to be Christians not only at our weekly service but also in all our lives.

This is the great need of our time: for the church to be the church. We need pastors who preach the whole counsel of God, and who train their people to know the gospel and the body of ethics and convictions that it animates. From there, we need ordinary Christians, people just like you and me, to speak up (Rom. 10), to act as salt and light (Matt. 5:13–16), and to love their neighbors (Luke 22:37). The church is told by secular culture today to be quiet, to muzzle its mouth, and to put its piety in a heart-shaped box, only taking it out on Sunday mornings. I want this book to encourage Christians to do exactly the opposite: to speak winsomely and with great conviction on behalf of gospel truth, biblical ethics, human dignity, and personal flourishing. This the church has done for two millennia; this it must do today.

In 2015, we do not know what the future holds. It is clear that we have witnessed the dawn of a new social order. Gay marriage is a cultural reality. Christian groups are getting kicked off college campuses. Pop culture has darkened in tone and morality. These are challenging times. Coming days may bring genuine hardship, even persecution, for American Christians. Or we may feature some ups and some downs, some great gains and some hard losses in the public square. The success of the pro-life cause over the years is just one example of how our country's narrative seems less predictable than it might be.

The kids are going to be all right. The millennials will hold the line on ethical issues. Sure, we regularly hear polling data that suggest otherwise. But if you had polled Americans in 1850 on the morality of slavery or in 1950 on the nature of civil rights, you likely would have been discouraged by the results. Cultures can shift. Views can change. Generations can wake up. As a millennial, I for one am tired of being told that my capitulation to secular culture is a foregone conclusion. It most certainly is not. I know that there are thousands, even millions, of people much like me. They will hold the line.

I firmly believe that there will be no truce on immorality. The true church will never surrender its convictions to the culture. It will never bow the knee to Caesar in slavish obedience. The church may suffer for being true to God. I am prepared for that, and we should all get ready for opposition and even persecution. But we will never give up the faith. We will not sell our beliefs for a cultural stew. I have written this book under this conviction. I believe that Chuck Colson would look us in the eye, take us by the hand, and tell us the same, were he present with us.

We are not here by accident. We have been called out for such a time as this. We are like Esther in days gone by. We find ourselves in the middle of a great societal contest taking place in the public square. The public square is the center of society in which all American citizens ask the great political and cultural questions of life and compete to give the most winsome and effective answers. We are not culture warriors, but there is indeed a competition of visions in modern America, and we have great answers to give. They can shape our culture for good. As Princeton professor Robert George said to me, "The future is not determined." We don't know what tomorrow will yield, in other words. Defeat is not assured. But much, it is clear, is at stake.

George went on to say, "In the public square, I don't want to play defense. I want to play offense." In other words, he wants to make a case, to persuade his fellow citizens to stand for life and truth and human dignity. Hearing George say this, I got chills. Later, I realized that he himself was similarly galvanized by a man who thrilled to take part in the great contest of ideas: Chuck Colson. Others had similar experiences with the man. For Robert George, Eric Metaxas, Timothy George, Congressman Frank Wolf, and countless others, Colson, as we will see in the following pages, had just this kind of inspiring effect.

It is my hope that his example, spelled out in this book, will have that effect on you. I want Colson to catalyze you to live with bold faith in a fractured age. Whether you counsel a young woman who feels abortion is the only way out of her personal nightmare, raise support to stop the sex trafficking of women in your county, or tell a classmate about the liberating gospel of Jesus, I want you to be like Colson and to be ready, as an ancient sage once said, to speak—but not only this. Like Colson, I want you to be ready to put steel in your words by acting courageously on them. This will mean, like Christ himself, that you must not expect applause for your witness, but that you be ready to sacrifice everything you have for the glory of God and the good of your neighbor.

These are momentous terms. This is a momentous time. Thankfully, we are not alone in this work. We have God at our side, and faithful examples who have gone ahead of us in his name. Their words and their examples still speak. And one of the most fruitful of those witnesses is Charles Wendell Colson.

ONE

ASCENT

Chuck Colson was sweating. He was standing just feet from the US president in his office. While Colson was perspiring, Richard Nixon was yelling. This happened often when his plans were frustrated. Nixon was not one to take setbacks lightly.

The president's request was simple: in fulfillment of a campaign pledge, he wanted a commission appointed to study Catholic schools. Though a Quaker, Nixon liked the Catholic model of education and, as the most powerful man in America, wished it to be studied at some length in order to publicly commend it. It was not a complex request, as far as presidential wishes go. But for various political reasons, Nixon's lead advisors had not acted to appoint the commission. Though America's chief executive must deal with ten thousand matters, at 5:00 p.m. on a Friday in the winter of 1970, this one had his full attention. Other aides were out of the office, but Colson was present. He was contemplating a relaxing Friday night when Nixon suddenly called him into his office.

"Chuck," Colson years later remembered him saying, "I

want a commission appointed *now.*" He paused and looked the thirty-eight-year-old staffer in the eye. "Break all the [expletive] china in this building," he roared, "but have an order for me to sign on my desk Monday morning."

With that, Colson was off. He ran back to his office, telling Joan Hall, his startled secretary, that he had no idea where to start. This was no easy mission to fulfill. It was a quiet Friday evening, the kind that features elite politicos fleeing their squeezed offices for ski slopes or coastal retreats, not digging in to meet the shouted expectations of world leaders. But Colson saw an opportunity, the kind his assertive nature craved. He hadn't had much to do since joining the White House some months earlier as Special Counsel to the President.

John Ehrlichman, chief domestic aide, and H. R. Haldeman, Chief of Staff, led Nixon's administration. The two men famously relished their roles as the president's gatekeepers. They had little interest in cultivating Colson, with his bullish personality and penchant for brilliant political strategy. The human heart in its natural state is not generous to competitors.

This was Colson's golden moment, however. The gatekeepers were temporarily away. Here was the world's preeminent leader not merely asking him to fulfill a request, but commanding him to do so, *ordering* him to do so. For a former Marine like Colson, this was irresistible stuff.

He set to work, finding the necessary documents to draft an executive order, placing call after call to various officials, even pulling the White House budget director from his faraway ski slope to approve the money to fund the commission. He worked furiously through the weekend over two "frantic" days, sleeping little, barely taking note of his family, in order to honor Nixon's request. On Monday morning, he placed the executive order on Nixon's desk. The work was done; the task was finished.[1]

The china was broken.

Chuck Colson had arrived.

———

The political overachiever did not hail from privilege. Charles "Chuck" Wendell Colson was born on October 16, 1931, in Winthrop, Massachusetts, just across the harbor from Boston. His parents, Wendell and Inez "Dizzy" Colson, raised Colson in upper-middle-class fashion despite lower-middle-class earnings. Dizzy was a force of nature with a classically extroverted personality. She was not adept, however, at managing family finances, a trait that created some chaos in the young man's life. The family struggled with debt and making ends meet, fostering anxiety in the household.

This was a plug-away era, though, and the Colsons did their part. Wendell devoted himself to what men of his generation took pride in: he put his head down and worked. He spent long hours in a meatpacking plant by day and took classes at Northeastern Law School by night to advance his family's prospects. Years later, Chuck would do the same while raising a young family. For a certain kind of child, the feeling of desperation produced by unstable finances creates a propulsive energy to succeed and strive. Colson's youthful experience left a mark on him, developing in him a desire to push ahead relentlessly despite tough odds. From eleven years of age, Chuck took summer jobs to defray his school expenses, which his father's salary barely covered.

Despite the family's humble beginnings, in 1945 Colson

was placed in a small but elite Boston prep school, Browne and Nichols (now called Buckingham Browne & Nichols, "BBN" for short). Located in Cambridge on the banks of the fabled Charles River, the school drew many of the children of Harvard faculty members, including some who could not gain admittance to the upper crust of the New England prep schools (Groton, Andover, and Phillips Exeter among them).

Colson's peers would go on to distinguish themselves, however. One year behind Colson was Anthony Perkins, the actor who would forever alter the American perception of roadside motels in *Psycho*. Mindy Kaling, beloved of *The Office*, is a more recent alum. In the years preceding Colson's arrival, the school had established a reputation for itself along calmer lines, winning the Thames Royal Regatta in London and vanquishing foes from larger Boston schools in athletic competitions.[2]

Colson fit the school's plucky mold well. He did not make his mark in sports, the dream of many a fifteen-year-old boy. Though he tried hard, Colson was an average athlete and a little heavyset for his age. But he had other, perhaps more potent, gifts: a forceful personality, the ability to rally peers to his cause of choice, and a quicksilver intellect. Colson worked his way onto the school newspaper, the *Spectator*, and quickly became its editor-in-chief. By 1948, the paper's advertising revenue had tripled under Colson's leadership.[3] His instincts for business and his interest in intellectual influence were nascent but growing. Even among a gifted peer group, Colson stood out. He was named the valedictorian of the forty-person senior class and voted "Most Likely to Succeed" by his classmates.[4] Little did they know just how well he would succeed.

Colson graduated from high school desiring an excellent

collegiate experience. After B&N, he applied to two Ivy League schools: Harvard and Brown, the latter located in Providence, Rhode Island. In what was his most remarkable coup to date, Colson won scholarships to both schools. This was the American dream, gift-wrapped and dazzling. Were Colson's life story to end at this point, his trajectory was already spectacular.

His paternal grandfather was a Swedish immigrant who died when Wendell was a teenager and his maternal grandfather was a British silversmith.[5] Neither side of the family had aristocratic connections. But Colson had an indomitable will. His application landed in the admissions office at Harvard Yard in a time when famed President James Bryant Conant (tenure from 1933 to 1953) effectively reshaped the storied institution, opening its famously restricted gates to students from diverse socioeconomic experiences.[6]

In an address given in 1940, Conant charged the American university to return to the educational ideals of Thomas Jefferson, who sought to enhance the intellectual life of all Americans, not just the upper class. More than a century after Jefferson, Conant sought an increasingly level playing field:

> I look forward to a future American society in which social mobility is sufficient to keep the nation in essence casteless—a society in which the ideals of both personal liberty and social justice can be maintained—a society which through a system of public education resists the distorting pressures of urbanized, industrialized life.[7]

Colson was a beneficiary of this expanded vision, though it is likely that his talent alone would have won him admission to Harvard. Colson, however, did not receive the news of his admission to the nation's most prestigious university with the customary awe and gratitude. Just the opposite: he turned Harvard down.

In his autobiography, *Born Again*, Colson reflected on how his humble origins clashed with the culture of Harvard. It was, he wrote, "pride" that drove him to sneer at his scholarship offer: "As a boy I used to stand on the pebbly beach looking across the gray-green waters of the harbor at the city then run by the Brahmins, the Beacon Hill establishment which traced its ancestry through generations of Harvard classes back to the *Mayflower*."[8]

Colson's rejection was an act of reverse snobbery. He and his family were not part of this hereditary aristocracy. They were "Swamp Yankees," as Colson noted, people who "fervently sought admission to the elite." But in his mind, he showed Harvard that he was not desperate for its stamp of achievement. When offered an entrée to the corridors of influence, a place at the table, Colson pushed back from it. He entered Brown on an ROTC scholarship and never looked back.

For a man who would focus on religious liberty, Brown University was a noteworthy choice. The school sits on College Hill, a high hill overlooking Providence, the city founded by Roger Williams in 1636 as a spiritual harbor for colonists whose polity and piety did not fit the dictates of Puritan New England. For this reason, many Baptists flocked to the city, establishing the first Baptist church in America midway up College Hill in 1638. More than a century later, Baptists chartered the College of Rhode Island in 1764 and settled it in its current location in 1770. The school was the third college founded in New England.[9] Its motto was *In Deo Speramus*—In God we hope.

By the time Colson matriculated at Brown in 1949, the cast of the university had changed dramatically. The school downplayed its evangelical heritage and featured a boisterous social scene. Colson joined a fraternity, Beta Theta Pi, founded at the school in 1848.[10] He threw himself into the social life of the outfit, hazing members, organizing escapades, and spending time with his girlfriend, Nancy Billings, a sweet young woman from an upper-crust New England family. The two dated throughout Colson's time at Brown and, as a result of Colson's irresistible wooing, were married in June 1953.[11]

Colson had already showed a penchant for aggressive thinking and an action-oriented philosophy. He continued in this vein at Brown, balancing his classes in political philosophy with his vibrant social life, student politics, and weekly drilling in uniform as a member of the Brown ROTC. Colson fit midcentury fraternity life to a tee. He smoked constantly (a habit that took him decades to drop), drank regularly, and galvanized those around him through his propensity for electric debates and organizational savvy. In a visit to Brown fifty years after his graduation in 1953, Colson reflected on how his environment shaped him:

The tolerance I was willing to fight for is the freedom in civil discourse in the public square to be able to present my truth claim and also listen respectfully to other people's truth claims. That is tolerance. Tolerance, I learned at Brown was to sit and listen respectfully while I disagreed with the person who was speaking, because we are in a free society, and I will die to protect his rights to speak freely about what he believes.[12]

As time wore on in Providence, Colson excelled in his studies in political philosophy, which featured an exciting array of thinkers. His classroom engagement with Nietzsche, Marx, and others trained him to relish the give-and-take of ideas, and the presence of classmates and professors who disagreed with him encouraged him to "listen respectfully." Later, he would launch a phase of his ministry centered around intellectual exchange.

Colson's training at Brown readied him for future endeavors. His academic preparation rendered him an unusual figure at times, for American evangelicals have had a rocky relationship with the life of the mind. Many Christians found themselves marginalized in elite academia in the early twentieth century. Some, in response, opted out of engagement with the secular academy, preferring instead to focus on practical ministry. In some evangelical circles, an attitude we could call "spiritual pragmatism" dominated.[13]

This was in sharp contrast to the past. In America, schools like Harvard, Yale, and Princeton (originally the College of New Jersey) represented colonial efforts to equip ministers with a love for Christ and for truth. The mottoes of these schools captured this desire: *Veritas Christo et Ecclesiae*, "Truth for Christ and the Church," at Harvard; *Lux et Veritas*, "Light and Truth," at Yale; *Dei Sub Numine Viget*, "Under the Protection of God She Flourishes," at Princeton. Today these schools are marked by their secularity, but they were each founded for a distinctly Christian purpose: to train young believers in a richly intellectual faith.

In 2015, when secularism looms large, evangelicals can give fresh priority to the life of the mind. In years past, Christians took it upon themselves to found colleges and universities that would pass down the faith and invigorate the heart and mind for Christ. This was founded in biblical conviction. In the language of Genesis, we should "take dominion" of all we can (1:26–27). The "dominion mandate," as it's called, does not only apply to our backyard gardens and our animal husbandry. It surely extends to all of life and all of our education, whether we study philosophical systems, multivariable calculus equations, or flagellum in a petri dish. Academic instruction reaped from faithful instructors at excellent institutions prepares us to think well in public, and to defend and promote the truth.

Colson began to enjoy the life of the mind at Brown. Engaging with various schools of thought excited him, as it would in later life. Though his early academic efforts were not stellar, Colson graduated *cum laude* from one of Brown's toughest departments. He later observed that, though he "read a lot of philosophy" at the university and "thought [he] understood it," it was not until his "life was turned upside down" and he "made a mess" of it that he really comprehended it.[14]

The young man enjoyed action as much as intellection. At this time in Brown's history, military officers held official faculty positions at Brown, training students in military strategy and theory. These subjects proved centrifugal for youth like Colson. Decades later, Colson identified the straight-back, shiny-shoed officer who first drew his interest in 1951 as "Lt. Cosgrove." The high standards and proud professionalism of the Marine Corps spoke to something deep in Colson. As often happens with college students, his idealistic side surged in him. Though acting like a boy with his fraternity buddies, he yearned to prove himself a man.

Cosgrove showed mastery in his dealing with Colson. He

played hardball with him, wondering aloud to Colson whether the would-be officer was "good enough" for the Marines.[15] Once again, Colson sat across a desk from an eminent man, a gatekeeper whose approval could shape the course of his life. Unlike his experience in Harvard Yard, however, Colson had no snappy retort for Cosgrove. He was speechless, a condition that did not often overtake him in his voluble life. But Cosgrove got Colson's attention. He threw himself into his ROTC exercises, seeking covertly to imitate the bearing and posture of Cosgrove. Not long after, in June 1953, he was commissioned an officer in the United States Marine Corps. He would later reflect that the moment in his ceremony in which he was first saluted as an officer was the proudest of his life.[16]

The Corps offered Colson a life of discipline and accountability, order and authority. It was led by legendary figures like famed three-star general "Chesty" Puller. In a tradition that raises certain heroic figures to Olympian heights, Puller stood out for his reputation for bravery and toughness. His famous dictums speak to the confidence of military officials of the period. At one point in Korea, facing tremendous fire, he told his men, "[T]hey're on our left, they're on our right, they're in front of us, they're behind us. They can't get away this time."[17] Such bravado led young patriots like Colson to follow Puller unquestioningly.

Colson never entered actual battle in the Korean War. By the time of his deployment, the conflict had ceased. Not surprisingly, Chuck found the peacetime military less appealing than the wartime military. He agitated to leave and begin a law career. But the military left a lasting impression on the young man. Amid his enjoyment of university life, Colson had found for the first time a cause he considered worth dying for, as he told students at his alma mater in 2003:

> When I went into the Marine Corps I was perfectly willing to lay my life down for the great opening words of the Declaration of Independence: "We hold these truths to be self-evident, that all men are created equal, that they are endowed by their Creator with certain unalienable rights, that among these are Life, Liberty and the pursuit of Happiness." That is a great thing. That is a great freedom![18]

Colson's patriotic zeal shows through five decades after his entrance into the Corps. Yet it is not his love of country that stands out. As captured by a seventy-two-year-old veteran, the idealistic young Marine was willing to die for a cause greater than his own interests. Colson knew already that the great end of life is to find something so precious, so all consuming, that it is worth even total sacrifice.

Colson did not stay a Marine for long. By 1955, two years after he entered the Corps, he won a spot on the navy's Junior Management Assistance program, an internship in Washington, DC, that served as an elevator to top governmental positions. Though Colson chafed at the quieter days of his life in the Corps, his identity as a Marine played a major role in his personal narrative. More than fifty years after his time of service, Colson would regularly describe himself in earlier years as a "tough Marine" who was humbled by a mighty God. His Marine heritage, in fact, seemed to play a larger role in his self-portrait than his Ivy League background. He was not made for a military career, but he was profoundly shaped by his experience in the armed forces.

Colson next moved on to the office of Raymond Fogler, the assistant secretary of the navy. Colson focused on procurement in his work, helping to assess the possible recipients of massive governmental contracts. As was becoming a pattern with the talented and impatient young man, he initially enjoyed his work. It did not take him long, however, to master his duties and perform proficiently in his job. Whenever this happened, as it generally did within a matter of months, his satisfaction plummeted. Colson was a classic executive, imbued with a type-A personality and a hunger for new challenges. He could not easily turn off his energy.[19]

During his time in DC, he became friends with staffers in the office of Massachusetts Senator Leverett Saltonstall, the highest-ranking Republican on the Senate Armed Forces Committee, the body responsible for decisions on defense contracts. "Salty," as he was known, hailed from a wealthy Boston family who, in classic twentieth-century fashion, summered in Maine, worshipped with the Unitarians, and graduated sons in bunches from Harvard. When the plum post of executive secretary opened up in the Boston Brahmin's office, Colson applied for it and was hired. He was twenty-five years old.

Colson was like a machine specially assembled for Washington. The young ex-Marine cut an impressive figure—over six feet tall, strong and standing straight, clad in the Brooks Brothers ensemble favored by many a graduate of elite prep schools. Colson took to the work at once, running Saltonstall's discombobulated outfit with aplomb, streamlining the staff and the office's operations. He was not intimidated by anyone and had a brain that never shut off.

Yet being the number two in a senator's office did not

satisfy Colson's peripatetic temperament. After he completed his twelve-hour workday with its constant preoccupations and ever-changing demands, he headed across town to the law school of George Washington University, not far from the US Department of State and famed lobbying zone K Street. Then Colson traveled home to Arlington, where he ate a hasty dinner before heading into his basement to study more law.[20]

The young politico's plate was more than full. On the domestic front, Chuck and Nancy had three children: Wendell (1954), Christian (1956), and Emily (1958). By all accounts, the children loved their father, who had charm to spare and could be delightful when not distracted. But with all that Colson had on his plate, it was hard to avoid distractions. Many a young father seeking to provide for his family and win a sense of vocational and financial stability knows these kinds of stresses.

These were exciting times for Colson, but as he made clear in later life, he struggled to balance the competing demands of work, education, and family. His ambition, impatience, and idealism formed a powerful stimulant. Colson would not have identified it as an idol at this point, but his career was overshadowing his other responsibilities. His meteoric rise continued, but this pattern would exact hard consequences in later years.

Colson was a complex individual. Even in this period, he defies easy stereotypes. The idealistic strain that compelled him to brave the harsh conditions of basic training to serve his country showed itself in quieter moments too. As Aitken recounted, Colson showed impressive compassion in 1956 to a man he didn't know when moving into the family's beautiful new home in Alexandria, Virginia. An older African American gentleman was moving stones on the Colson property to build a new patio when he suddenly collapsed. According to the social and racial codes of the day, Colson had no need to help the man. This was 1956, when Virginia Senator Harry Byrd convinced more than one hundred congressmen from Southern states to sign an anti-integrationist document entitled "The Southern Manifesto on Integration." The state of Virginia even passed a formal resolution based on this manifesto in 1956, attempting an end around the Supreme Court's pro-integration decision in the 1954 *Brown v. Board of Education* case.

In such an unjust climate, no one would have batted an eye had Colson yelled at the mover. He did the opposite. He brought the man inside and personally attended to him until he recovered. Aitken noted that "the other workmen stood gaping with astonishment" due to the unusual nature of Colson's response.[21] Long before the purpose of his life became caring for the forgotten of society, Colson had an inherent interest in helping others weaker than him. He crossed racial boundaries easily, a trait that mattered hugely in his later career, and that made him friends everywhere he went.

Pride ruled Colson's life in this period. But even in his pre-converted life, he did not think of himself as better than other people. Coming to faith would bring these instincts to full flourishing, but they were already present in him. Chuck Colson always had an instinct for justice and a desire to serve in practical ways. It never left him.

Such character always leaves a powerful impression. Not long ago, I was deplaning after a long flight. One of the pilots walked ahead of me on the gangway and stooped to pick up a candy wrapper. There was no one else around; he didn't look to see if anyone noticed his good deed. He just put the wrapper in his pocket and walked on, posture straight as an arrow. This demonstration of character reminded me of the essential nature of leadership. Pilots are leaders, after all. They have tremendous responsibilities. This pilot was adept at his job, but he clearly did not think too highly of himself.

There is a profound lesson here for young evangelicals who wish to be leaders. It is not our talent that will matter most. It is our character, our God-shaped morality. If we live in virtue, then nothing the world throws at us can touch us. If we compromise our ethics, however, we set ourselves up for failure. Character is not only a set of practices, though. It is a mind-set. It is a posture of humility motivated by the recognition that we *should* be humble. Leaders of the Christlike kind, in fact, see that leadership is humble at its core. We put others before ourselves in acting for the corporate good. This is not only a high-minded way of life, but a cruciform one (Phil. 2:1–11).

Soon after this episode, Senator Saltonstall appointed his young staffer to be his campaign manager for his 1960 reelection effort. Colson threw himself into the work. He had worked on campaigns for more than a dozen years and knew the practicalities of winning elections. His task as Saltonstall's campaign manager was not a small one, however. Massachusetts boasted a young political star named John F. Kennedy. As a young Democrat with a bright future, Kennedy would only help the prospects of fellow candidates, including Foster Furcolo, former governor of Massachusetts and Saltonstall's Democratic challenger for his Senate seat.

Colson pulled out all the stops in the race, creating shadow committees to suggest bipartisan endorsement of Saltonstall, marshaling dozens of volunteers to send out carefully crafted mailings, and diverting outspoken critics of his shrewd political style. In the end, his efforts prevailed. Saltonstall won the race and offered him a position in his office. Colson turned it down.[22]

In 1960, Colson yet again took on a massive challenge and conquered it. He served as the mastermind of the reelection of a genteel and somewhat detached Republican senator in a state that voted Democrat. This was by any measurement a career-making accomplishment. It could have allowed Colson—still not even forty years of age—to settle into a comfortable role as a DC politico. Whenever tranquility dawned in Colson's life, however, his adrenaline intervened.

Instead of taking a cushy position in either Washington or any number of top Boston law firms, Colson decided to partner with a friend named Charles Morin to found his own law practice in his hometown. Colson and Morin struggled through several years of instability before landing a number of lucrative accounts with large businesses and firms. Once again, Colson had made the seemingly impossible materialize: Colson & Morin became not only solvent but also successful.[23] In law, as in politics, as in education, Colson excelled.

All this achievement came at a cost. As noted earlier, Colson's commitments took him away from his family and led to estrangement between him and his wife, Nancy. In January 1964, the two were divorced. Later in the year Colson married Patty Hughes, a staffer in the Saltonstall office. This period was one of the toughest of Colson's life. For the rest of his life, he regretted the pain he caused his family. Colson never justified his actions or downplayed them. Though he did not wish to continually revisit his divorce, he made clear when he did speak or write of it that it spoke to his hardness of heart.

Colson's travails did not stop his forward momentum. He kept his political hat in the ring, attending the 1964 GOP Convention in Miami. He developed a relationship with Vice President Richard Nixon, who had failed in his earlier bid for the presidency. Colson was not sanguine about the prospects of Republican candidates in the mid-60s; he worked behind closed doors to gin up a new Nixon candidacy. He did so while running a rapidly growing law firm that required him to shuttle up and down the East Coast. The pull was familiar even if the challenge was new and even bigger than usual: Colson wanted to be a part of a Nixon administration, were there to be one. He wanted not merely to be proximate to power but to plunge into the very center of it: the American presidency.

The runway to the White House for Colson was not a long one. He served as codirector of the Key Issues Committee for Nixon during his presidential run in 1968, helping to develop and articulate the candidate's policy stances.[24] The post was a crucial one, and when Nixon was elected to the presidency in November 1968, Colson became a household name. *TheWall Street Journal* published a lengthy front-page profile of him, which resulted in skyrocketing business for the law firm and the offer, in 1969, of the post of assistant secretary of state in charge of legislative affairs.[25] Colson turned it down, adding this position to a list of others declined following the successful campaign. Then, in the fall of 1969, Colson received the call that he coveted: the president of the United States of America summoned him to the Oval Office. Colson recalled the moment of a lifetime in *Born Again*:

> As I stepped for the first time into the sun-filled, stark-white, curving walled room, my heart was beating so hard

I wondered if it could be heard. I walked over a huge blue and gold oval-shaped rug, the Great Seal of the United States colorfully embroidered in its center, directly beneath a matching white plaster seal molded in the ceiling. In front of the floor-to-ceiling windows looking out across the South Lawn, the President sat at a large mahogany desk.

The Harvard dean. Lieutenant Cosgrove. And now, Colson sat across from the "single most important man in the world," the American president. The experience was intoxicating. Nixon offered Colson the position of Special Counsel, which Colson did not turn down.

One can hardly overplay the poignancy of this moment. Colson's grandparents had struggled in their adopted country. His parents had little money to spare. Stress was a regular part of Chuck's childhood, so he worked his way to the top at Browne & Nichols. Then he did the same at Brown, in Saltonstall's Senate office, in Boston law, and now in the executive branch of DC politics. At thirty-eight he was rich, successful, and wanted. The underdog had beaten his competitors. It was the classic American success story.

Because Colson's star rose so quickly, his coming fall would be spectacular. Yet none of Colson's experiences, successes, and trials would be wasted. His future ministry was directly affected by the events of his early life. His humble beginnings and immigrant heritage allowed him to form meaningful connections with people who felt estranged from the success culture of elite American life. His ability to not only survive but also stand out amid patrician peers equipped him to navigate the halls of power with finesse and confidence. His credentials from excellent New

England institutions gave him access to conversations not easily entered by others. To the end of his life, these traits would prove invaluable to Colson and his causes.

These were not his only strengths, of course. Over the years, Chuck Colson learned the art of "breaking fine china." Colson's combination of will, talent, and idealism spurred him to seek out challenges and then do whatever it took to finish the task. One thread remained in full throughout coming days: whenever needed, Chuck Colson did his duty to the full.

———

The man who stood before Nixon as he shouted his orders passed his initial test. He may have perspired throughout his time under Nixon. Then and later, he found the capacity to get things done, to push past whatever low expectations had been set. This aspect of Colson's life should profoundly encourage Christians today. Whether or not we have presidents calling us into the office for job offers, we can recognize that God has led and is leading every facet of our lives. He will use all of us, including even our sinful pasts, for his glory. Nothing that has happened in our lives needs to be wasted. Even before our conversions, God prepared us for work in his kingdom.

Colson's example also reminds us that no one is God-proof. To this point in his story, Colson had carved out a remarkable life for himself. He beat the odds, became a success, and found his way to the top. He had precious little time for religion or spiritual things; his life was oriented in a thoroughly secular direction. Like it is for all of us outside of Christ, his life was based around him. But though Colson tried to live a self-sufficient life, he ultimately would not be able to pull it off. No person can write God out of his existence. It will not work.

Even as Colson ignored God, God was charting his course. There is infinite wisdom in divine providence, and there is infinite potential in divine grace. Colson's past was not an accident. Our pasts are not accidents. The challenge before us today is to recognize the hand of God in all our lives and to view ourselves not as hindered by our histories but as prepared by providence for whatever the future may hold. This includes our immediate circumstances, but also the sinful past we all have. God does no evil, but he will use even our sinful pasts for his purposes. There is no more shocking discovery one can make in biblical teaching, but no more encouraging one, either.

Colson would later use his energy and his vision to great effect as a Christian. His political experience and strategic bent prepared him for leadership in the church. The same is true of us and our experience and strengths. What has God done in our lives that can be redeemed and used in service of him? Considering this question takes us off the sidelines, admiring the great figures of the past, all too certain of our own short-comings. It puts us squarely into the middle of things, and restores our agency and responsibility. The past cannot be altered. The future, on the other hand, has yet to be molded.

In 1969, for Colson, the future seemed very bright indeed.

TWO

CONVERSION

Chuck Colson was weeping. Not muffled crying—these were wracking sobs. The man whose life revolved around political theater, the need to perform and posture in order to gain position, was not acting. He was distraught.

This was not normal for a man who lived his life from strength to strength. By the time he was forty, Colson had amassed an enviable chest of life victories won by his blend of bravado, determination, and talent. He was not driven only by conquest. Colson was a conservative, a man who followed his gut, and a patriot to the point that he would die for his country.

Colson was also motivated by a powerful sense of pride. He wanted to get ahead. He wanted to win. Specifically, he wanted his enterprises and projects and candidates to win, and he went well beyond expectations in this pursuit. This was especially true in Colson's role as Special Counsel to President Richard Nixon, a role he filled from 1969 to 1973. As time and countless newspaper articles would show, Colson was willing to go the extra mile to support and propel Nixon. He cut corners, bruised feelings, and did whatever was necessary in his eyes to fulfill his duty to the president.

Colson was not amoral by any stretch, and later press coverage would exaggerate his role in the Watergate affair. Yet here was the essential reality: Colson fit the stereotype of the Nixon White House in the early 1970s. He was a shrewd, successful, and tough political operator. He was fearless, he idealized Nixon, and like the ex-Marine that he was, he went to great lengths to meet and exceed the charge given him by his leader.

Colson was by no means the key participant in numerous unsavory schemes that later came to light. He was, however, a vital and outspoken part of the Nixon administration. This led, in the mid-1970s, to his professional undoing. It also prompted this moment in his car on the road to Dover, Massachusetts, in which for the first time he realized that before the bar of divine justice, he was guilty.

———

In Colson's early years at the White House, he filled a variety of roles. Colson was not simply a fixer, however. He was an insightful political strategist, adept at building alliances on behalf of his boss that not only won temporary victories but also signaled the course of future political maneuvering. Nixon knew he had drawn an unusually gifted staffer in Colson. Years after Watergate, he recalled Colson's devotion and political skill in his autobiography:

> He worked on policy matters with energy and devotion.
> He spent hours with labor groups, veterans' organizations,

ethnic minorities, and religious groups. He was positive, persuasive, smart, and aggressively partisan. His instinct for the political jugular and his ability to get things done made him a lightning rod for my own frustrations at the timidity of most Republicans in responding to attacks from the Democrats and the media. When I complained to Colson I felt confident that something would be done, and I was rarely disappointed.[1]

One major aspect of Colson's program in Nixon's first term was to build bridges with organized labor. Unions had historically leaned Democratic and presented a perennial problem for conservatives. When many Republicans wrote off labor as a lost demographic cause, Colson sensed an opportunity. Vietnam had unsettled America and created tension between blue-collar workers and blue-hearted politicians. The workers sided with the soldiers and believed in the rightness of the conflict while the politicians who had historically enjoyed their votes sided against the war.

Colson seized on this combustible situation, wooing prominent union leaders and inviting them to the White House to meet with Nixon. It took time to build trust between Nixon and major groups like the Teamsters, but Colson's work paid off prior to the 1972 presidential election when the incumbent won the endorsement of the fabled organization.[2] In the national race, Colson helped engineer a stunning 20 percent increase in votes among union members and their families.[3] This bloc targeting helped Nixon win a second presidential term.

There is a lesson here for young evangelicals. In an age dominated by social media, it can be tempting to opt out of the hard work of cause building. Real change comes when Christians put skin in the game. Chuck Colson was not at this time a believer, but he knew that political victories required careful thinking, serious discipline, and unwavering commitment. If you wanted to win an election and thereby set the political tone for the country, you had to pay the price. You had to put boots on the ground.

These are important words for young Christians to ponder. We're in the age of easy activism, *slacktivism* as some have called it. Why get involved in a campaign when you can just post a status on Facebook promoting your favorite cause? Why sacrifice, risk commitment, and cost yourself lots of free time—"me time"—when you could just give to Kickstarter and call it a day? Social media involvement is great—even important. But we should not miss how it can leave us disconnected from the gritty aspects of public-square witness.

Colson's political work in this period was not lily white. We don't want to emulate the less savory aspects of the operators of the Nixon White House. But we do want to recognize in our time that evangelicals need to practice a chastened form of *realpolitik*. If we are going to see real legal and legislative change in our country, we need activists and workers who will persevere in high-pressure settings to advance righteousness and oppose injustice. This is not an easy call. It is a meaningful one, however.

The stakes are high. If those who stand for life and marriage and the family and the goodness of religious institutions are outworked and outvoted, we should expect to see our society deteriorate. If our vision of flourishing is not driven by serious personal and political investment, we should plan on other visions of flourishing winning the hearts and minds of our neighbors. Well before his conversion, Chuck Colson understood this. In our day, we should too.

Colson was a brilliant political strategist. He was also disciplined and hardworking. In these respects, he was an impressive figure. But the Nixon White House asked him to use his tougher instincts too. When a former employee of the administration named Daniel Ellsberg released the "Pentagon Papers," highly classified documents revealing secrets of American involvement in Vietnam, the White House rocked with fury. Long before Julian Assange, Ellsberg captured the attention of the nation by leaking secure documents crucial to American diplomacy. Nixon, as one might expect, was furious. He called Colson in and directed him to have Ellsberg exposed as the troublemaker Nixon believed him to be.[4] Colson complied, opening fire on him in the press while he oversaw a full-scale research effort into his life.

The leaks did not stop, however. Nixon remained furious and demanded further attention. As a result, the White House staff took the fateful step of adding ex-CIA operative Howard Hunt to their covert team. An alumnus of Brown like Colson, Hunt was hired to do research on the Pentagon Papers. Soon, though, he became part of a shadow unit called the "Plumbers," operating from deep within the White House, that would take action to stop the release of state secrets. Though Colson recruited Hunt to the president's staff, Hunt reported to John Ehrlichman and had no contact with Colson.[5] Hunt worked with G. Gordon Liddy on his assignments, which only a handful of staff knew about. So it was that a random phone call in June 1972 took Colson by surprise.[6]

Colson had heard about a news story regarding a robbery earlier that day in the Democratic National Committee at the Watergate office complex in Washington. He thought little of it, however, until none other than Ehrlichman called him at home on a Saturday. It turned out that one of the robbers had a piece of paper with Hunt's name on it. This seemed ludicrous to Colson—surely, he thought to himself, Hunt hadn't cooked up something so reckless as a robbery in his effort to oppose the president's enemies. But Hunt had done exactly that. Though Colson, Nixon, and the rest of the administration could not have known it then, this would prove to be the little fox that would spoil an entire presidential vineyard.

The media soon awoke. Led by the *Washington Post*, the press picked up on the story and tied it to the Nixon administration.[7] The White House staff expected the story would do some temporary damage and then blow over, as small scandals tended to. Colson himself had plenty to concentrate on, namely, getting Nixon reelected over George McGovern, his Democratic challenger. By late summer, the election was less than three months away and the effort required every second of Colson's energy and savvy.

It was at this point that Colson decided to issue a staff directive that soon went viral. In a huff over the Watergate coverage, Colson doubled down. He dictated a memo that informed his staff that they were not to leave the city until after the election. He reiterated his single-mindedness and then affirmed a reporter's characterization from a week-old story: "Last week's UPI story that I was once reported to have said that 'I would walk over my grandmother if necessary' is absolutely accurate."[8]

At this point, Colson had not said that he would "walk over his grandmother" to serve the president. This bracing line, which became one of the twentieth century's most enduring political quotes, was originally stated by a commenter in a *Wall Street Journal* article a year earlier. It had not been Colson's line until this fitful moment, when he owned it in full. The memo was leaked almost immediately and found column space in media across the world.

Nothing about this saying damned Colson politically. Far from it: this was the kind of defiance that the Nixon political machine thrived on. However, the self-description would come back to haunt Colson in spades when the criminal deeds of the Nixon-era White House became known. It made Colson an easy target as the ruthless rule breaker of Nixon's staff. In actuality, Colson was more scrupulous than numerous White House associates, including several who had a good deal more power than he. But because he was bold and took pleasure in giving his opponents no quarter, he would be spared little hostility when Watergate exploded.

At this point, we need to quickly recount the events centering around Watergate. One of the most frequently discussed affairs of the twentieth century, much confusion surrounds the affair and, even to the current day, various misunderstandings about the roles of Colson and others persist. In late summer 1971, the "Plumbers" burglarized the Los Angeles offices of a psychiatrist, seeking information on Ellsberg. In June 1972, the *Post* broke the story about the burglary in the same month of the offices of the Democratic National Committee. The intent of the burglary, it soon became clear, was the bugging of the offices so that the White House could eavesdrop on its political rivals. In November 1972, Nixon won reelection to the presidency, despite leading a country fractured by debate over the conflict in Vietnam. In March 1973, Colson resigned his post as Special Counsel due to a desire to step away from the grind of politics and to return to Colson and Shapiro, his law firm.[9]

During this time—from roughly February 1971 through June 1973—Nixon was also secretly taping conversations and telephone calls in multiple locations. These included the Oval Office, his office in the Old Executive Office Building, the Cabinet Room, and Camp David. The tapes run nearly eleven thousand hours. Presidential taping was not in fact new; it began under Franklin Delano Roosevelt and has continued to the current day under Barack Obama. The Nixon tapes are unique because they were activated by voice and feature conversation revolving around the Nixon administration's immoral activities.

Around this same time, media coverage of Watergate and the possibly corrupted Nixon White House reached fever pitch. In late spring 1973, *Post* reporters Bob Woodward and Carl Bernstein suggested in print that Colson knew about Watergate (he did not). In April 1973, Colson took a lie detector test to prove his innocence on the matter of Watergate planning.[10] During this same time, press coverage intimated that Colson had overseen the bugging, a charge that was not true but gained considerable traction due to his hard-driving reputation. In late April, key members of the Nixon inner circle—Haldeman, Ehrlichman, and Attorney General Richard Kleindienst—resigned due to intense scrutiny of the Watergate controversy. Shortly thereafter, a team of prosecutors who were appointed to trace wrongdoing among the president's team exonerated Colson.

As spring 1973 turned into summer, Colson breathed a sigh of relief. He continued his dogged defense of Nixon, believing the president had no part in Watergate. At this point, the worst was yet to come. In 1973, the *Washington Post* reported that Colson wanted the left-leaning Brookings Institution to be firebombed in order to obtain lost documents. Colson had said no such thing; White House investigator Jack Caulfield talked with Colson about the documents, and Caulfield mentioned the possibility of creating a diversion by fire at Brookings in order to retrieve the documents. Colson then told Caulfield, "I don't know how you're going to do it, but all I know is that the president wants those papers back."[11] In 2002, Caulfield apologized to Colson for spreading the rumor through John Dean that Colson had ordered a bombing.[12]

Though Colson sought to set the record straight in different settings, he could only do so much. This was especially true when the press ran stories in mid-June about the secret White House tape-recording system. Colson apparently learned about the taping system the same day millions of other Americans did. Watergate had already cost a number of very powerful figures their careers. The country was abuzz over it, allegations of illegality and slander flew back and forth between parties, and the American presidency hung in the balance. Chuck Colson had long relished being in the middle of it all. Now, being hammered in the press, he found himself desperate for solace.[13]

On August 12, 1973, Chuck and Patty left Washington for New England. They wanted to go to one of their favorite vacation spots on the Maine coast, a manner of retreat that had served them on numerous occasions. They drove to Colson's family's home in Dover, Massachusetts, where Colson left Patty to go on a trip of his own.[14] He wanted to see his friend Tom Phillips, president of Raytheon, then the state's largest company. Three technological entrepreneurs had founded Raytheon in 1922.

Initially, the company grew through its manufacture of radio tubes, but in the years of World War II it became well known and highly profitable through its production of radar and guidance systems. Phillips started as an engineer and quickly rose through the ranks, becoming president in the 1960s and leading the company to newfound heights. By the early 2000s, a decade after Phillips retired, the company started with $50,000 in seed money had become an $18 billion Fortune 500 entity.[15]

Phillips found himself in the flush of this success when Colson came calling in August 1973. He knew that his friend Chuck was navigating a tough stretch of life. He had already told Chuck about his recent conversion at a Billy Graham crusade. Despite his incredible success—becoming president of Raytheon at age forty—Phillips knew that he had nothing outside of Christ. He was in an ideal position to speak with Colson, who was himself remarkably accomplished but internally hollow.

Over iced tea, Colson and Phillips talked about their lives, Tom walking through his newfound faith for his religiously uninterested friend. "I saw what was missing," Tom said regarding the Graham event, and it was "the personal relationship with Jesus Christ, the fact that I hadn't ever asked Him into my life, hadn't turned my life over to Him."[16] There at Madison Square Garden, the serious businessman was converted to Christ. Christ played in ten thousand places, including the home of the New York Knicks.

This was an unusual moment for both men. To this point in his life, Colson had only experienced flickers of interest in religious things. He felt stirred while standing on the deck of a warship gazing at a vast ocean, holding his children, or debating religion in a lunchtime conversation. You could call such instances natural revelation—a person feeling instinctively what is essentially true, albeit without a broader theological framework. One senses a greater purpose to life, a massive design in the cosmos and in the narrative of one's own existence, but has little context by which to figure it all out.

During the conversation, Phillips did not hold back in sharing the "good news" with his friend. A key part of his witness was his discussion of sin. Not sin in the abstract—sin as a personal force and a crime against a holy God. This is what scared Colson that night. As the two men talked about faith and Colson's struggles with Watergate, Tom stopped Chuck in his tracks. He did not allow his persuasive friend to airbrush his failures or explain them away. He spoke directly to him: "Chuck, I hate to say this, but you guys brought it on yourselves. If you had put your faith in God, and if your cause were just, he would have guided you. And his help would have been a thousand times more powerful than all your phony ads and shady schemes put together."[17]

This was not the way that associates generally spoke to Colson. But the truthfulness of Tom's words crashed into his defensive heart. Thrown off balance, Chuck listened as Tom read to him from a worn copy of C. S. Lewis's *Mere Christianity*. The section was on pride: "In God you come up against something which is in every respect immeasurably superior to yourself. Unless you know God as that—and, therefore, know yourself as nothing in comparison—you do not know God at all. As long as you are proud you cannot know God."[18] This was devastating stuff.

As he pondered those words, Colson saw his sin for the first time. Pride dominated his heart. It had eroded his morals and his judgment. Colson had not committed the major crimes of which he was accused. He had, however, bent the rules for years, stooping to heavy-handed and sometimes morally dubious tactics to win elections and advance his bosses' prospects. His whole life, it seemed, was one long exercise in pride, in winning, in getting ahead, and in getting back at his adversaries. Chuck had not directed the Watergate break-in. He had, however, allowed pride to sand down his judgment. He was, in sum, guilty.

Tom and Chuck continued to converse for some time. Before Colson left, Tom urged him to "accept Christ" as his Savior. Colson put him off, but Tom did not force the issue. He prayed a powerful prayer, asking the Lord to open Colson's heart. After closing pleasantries, Colson reflected thirty-five years later to the day that he "left his house that night shaken by the words he had read from C. S. Lewis's *Mere Christianity* about pride. It felt as if Lewis were writing about me, former Marine captain, Special Counsel to the President of the United States, now in the midst of the Watergate scandal. I had an overwhelming sense that I was unclean."[19]

For the first time, Colson saw his existence in God-centered terms. He now recognized that he was not a "good person," as one naturally thinks. He was a sinner, accountable to a holy God who had created him and given him all he had. Yet to this point, Chuck had not thanked his Creator, nor sought to know him and honor him. He had instead ignored God, shutting out the central truth of life. This amounted not simply to neglect. It left Chuck "unclean," a remarkable summation. God was holy; Chuck was not. He was shot through with pride, condemned by his sinfulness, and without any hope of his own.

Here was a crisis Colson could not solve. There was no explanation to give. There was no story to plant. There were no political wheels to turn. Chuck Colson, forty-two years of age, famous the country over, wealthy and accomplished, the conqueror of a challenging background and too many other trials to count, had come to the end of himself. The sense of the divine had once been a flicker. Now it was a blinding light, enveloping Colson, exposing him, undoing him. The gentle but straightforward witness of a friend, bolstered by Lewis's meditations, had brought Chuck face-to-face with God.

As Colson considered his sin, he wept so hard that he could not drive. As he wrote thirty-five years later, "I was crying too hard—and I was not one to ever cry. I spent an hour calling out to God. I did not even know the right words. I simply knew that I wanted Him. And I knew for certain that the God who created the universe heard my cry." These were not tears of "sadness," however, but "tears of relief."[20] As Colson cried, he prayed, over and over, *Take me.* The man who had evaded even the thought of the Almighty now begged to be his possession.

Conversion did not come quietly to Chuck Colson. This was a "Damascus road" experience in Dover, Massachusetts. His conversion upended his life, changed his priorities, and reoriented his interests. Decades later at an event at Gordon College honoring Tom Phillips, the former "hatchet man" described his new life in Christ. "Thirty-six years ago, in a flood of tears, my life was transformed," Colson said. Addressing his old friend, Colson queried rhetorically, "What do you say to someone who saved your life? I will continue to serve Christ as long as I have breath." In his view, he would not have drawn breath for nearly as long as he did without faith in the Son of God: "And if I managed somehow to survive the high-powered party life in Washington among the rich, famous, and powerful, I would have been so miserable I don't think I could have lived with myself. If I did not know for sure that the God who created us sent His Son to die on a cross that my sins might be forgiven, I would have long ago suffocated in the stench of my own sin."[21]

Chuck Colson was not ruined by Watergate. He was ruined by the gospel of Jesus Christ, which hunted him like a hound of heaven and claimed him when he was at his most vulnerable. He was not looking for God, but God was looking for him. Colson did not simply check the box beside the name "Jesus Christ" on a list of religious options and then go about his life. As he pondered the weight of this event, he saw that he had to turn away from his old self. He had to renounce devious ways. He was forced, most of all, to look his pride in the face. He had a heart of darkness, and his only hope was divine grace.

For several days, Colson wrestled with this decision. On the Maine coast, he reckoned with the person and work of Jesus Christ.[22] He delved into Scripture and saw that the sins of mankind had cost Christ his life, for he bore them on the cross. From this point until the day in 2012 when he collapsed while speaking on a stage, it was Christ and the hope of grace that compelled him.

Like Paul, Colson had discovered the reason the Lord put him on earth: to work for a heavenly kingdom, not an earthly one. For the rest of his life, words that many Christians understand from a distance—"my kingdom is not of this world"—would remind Colson of just how invested he once was in the American presidency. Though he had ascended all the way to the top, Colson saw that he had chosen the wrong kingdom.

When Colson returned to his home, he found an environment boiling with anger. Throughout this time, Patty was by his side, supportive and as bewildered by the events at hand as he was. As 1973 wore on, he was called to testify before congressional committees about Watergate. In August 1973, one of the prosecutors investigating Nixon's staff struck fear in Colson's heart by warning him of an impending indictment for criminal activity. Colson had gotten tangled up in the Watergate break-in by passing on money that was ultimately used to fund the crime. He testified under oath that he had not known the purpose of this money, only that it was destined for purposes of national security.[23] Others confirmed his lack of direct involvement in Watergate, and Colson was not indicted.

But the prosecuting team wanted blood. They told Colson that he would have to admit to guilt for conspiring on the break-in. In reality, this would result only in a legal slap on the wrist. Colson would admit to a felony. It was a simple if painful proposal. Colson would have to fudge history a bit and confess to knowledge he had not possessed. He would also have to cooperate with prosecutors to bring other Nixon administration officials down.[24]

Here, just days after his conversion, was a fork in the road. The easier way out of Colson's troubles involved confessing to criminal activity he had not done, but then moving on from the whole mess as a free man. The tougher way meant not confessing to the uncommitted crime, which was morally less complex for Colson but meant the prosecutors would dial up the heat on him due to his unwillingness to help them land charges against other White House officials. Colson, buoyed by the support of his family, rejected the plea-bargain deal.

Soon after, in March 1974, Colson pleaded "not guilty" to the indictment. Three months later at his arraignment for sentencing, however, Colson changed his plea. On June 21, 1974, he pled guilty to a charge crafted, oddly enough, by his own lawyer.[25] During the three-month period between hearings, Colson came to see that though he had not played the role of Watergate mastermind alleged by the press, he nonetheless had acted immorally in targeting Daniel Ellsberg. His decision to stand trial on this account shocked many of his friends, including his newfound peers in the "Fellowship," a small prayer group run by a man named Doug Coe. But Colson would not turn back. He pled guilty to obstruction of justice and accepted the fact that he might well be sentenced to prison for doing so.

The formal charge against Colson was as follows:

In July and August 1971, the defendant Charles W. Colson endeavored to and did release defamatory and derogatory allegations concerning one of the attorneys engaged in the legal defense of Daniel Ellsberg for the purpose of publicly disseminating the said allegations the known and probable consequences of which would be to influence, obstruct, and impede the conduct and outcome of the criminal prosecution of Daniel Ellsberg.[26]

On these grounds—attempting to obstruct justice—Colson stood trial in late June 1974. He faced this frightening prospect with his family by his side, the support of numerous friends, and most importantly, the conviction that God held his life in his hands.

This dramatic story speaks to us today. Colson's accomplishments under Nixon show us that while earthly work is valuable, nothing that is done for our own glory will last. We can be anonymous, or we can be profiled on the front page of the *Wall Street Journal*. In the end, all our kingdom building for our own renown will crumble. Colson saw this firsthand as the Nixon administration detonated before his eyes, sweeping his career away.

Colson's conversion speaks to the miraculous nature of our own spiritual lives. He did not become perfect when the Lord saved him. He fought pride the rest of his life and, with his heady achievements and proximity to cultural influence, knew that he fell victim to it throughout his life. But he made a break with this sin when he was born again. The gospel message of Jesus Christ's atoning death and life-giving resurrection rescued Chuck Colson from destruction. It did not tweak his practices; it did not rearrange his ethics. It ruined him and remade him.

So it is for us. We may never have fully realized the power of our conversions. But we, too, are remade. We are each a new creation (2 Cor. 5:17). Because of this, we are each a force for good in the world. We don't need a presidential appointment. Right now, wherever we are, the power of our conversions enables us to overcome sin and to advance the gospel in our world. We are not spectators. We are participants in the great work of redemption—every one of us.

A key part of this work is preaching the gospel. In sharing the good news of Jesus Christ with our friends, we are not calling them to a life-improvement seminar. We're announcing the possibility of radical conversion. This is not a comfortable fact for many. The human heart naturally craves a tame and manageable spirituality. The world rewards such respectable religion, which gives no offense and asks for no transformation. But this is not biblical faith. As Colson discovered, conversion to Christ means that ambitions have to change or die, desires must be repented of and reoriented, and some behaviors have to stop altogether. This is what it means to embrace the full-orbed gospel.

This is incredibly freeing for Christians. We are no longer responsible for image maintenance and brand promotion. We've given up on any project of self-aggrandizement, of making ourselves look impressive. In Jesus, we have lost it all. The worst has happened to us: God has exposed us as sinners, convicting us of our evil beyond a shadow of a doubt. But the punishment for our sin has not fallen on us. Christ took it upon himself at the cross. Through faith in his blood, we are freed from sin and guilt and hell and condemnation (Rom. 6:6; 8:9–11). We know the joy of fellowship with the risen Messiah. This is life, true life.

In our conversion we become a "new creation" in Christ (2 Cor. 5:17). This means that we have a new identity, a new self-understanding, a new daily experience. The central truth about us is brand-new. We have taken on the name "Christian," and lost the name "sinner," which we once did so much to deserve. This is not to say, of course, that conversion means we stop sinning. Peter, for example, denied Jesus (John 18). We must regularly "put off" the old nature, confessing and repenting of our sins. We must also "put on" the new nature, consciously living according to God's will (Col. 3:1–11).

In this sense, all believers are something like former alcoholics. We are not mastered by our sin. We are each a new person. We have broken with our old selves and their old practices. But we still hear the serpent's whisper in our ears, and we sadly fall at times. In such moments, Satan would have us believe that we are still trapped, but he lost all power to mislead us when Christ defeated him at the cross. God's grace has triumphed not only in the cosmos but also in our lives.

The newness of the Christian's identity is wondrous, even strange, in a world that yearns for redemption but struggles to believe in it. Even as we share that spiritual transformation is possible, we need to take care to communicate that following Jesus is not quiet. It is not predictable. It is not "safe." Christ does not promise us that he will make our lives easier. Coming to faith may actually make our daily lives more complicated. Jesus will take us places we never imagined.

This was certainly true for Chuck Colson. The first place God called him to go, after all, was prison.

THREE

PRISON

Chuck Colson was afraid. Clad in his familiar Brooks Brothers suit, he paced the floor. He was unsure about this visit. It scared him in a way others did not.

Talking with inmates was not a new experience for Colson. By this time in his ministry career, he had entered thousands of prisons and spoken to thousands of prisoners. Over and over again, Colson had gone into jails, venturing boldly into places many Christians wanted to pretend did not exist.

Despite Colson's boldness, this visit was a tough one. This was unusual because the prisoner in question was not a six-foot-six-inch gangbanger but a tiny, physically harmless shoplifter. Her name was Bessie Shipp. An African American woman, she sat by herself in a rocking chair, far from other prisoners, shivering, a blanket wrapped around her, as Colson later recalled.[1] Bessie was alone not because of bad behavior in the jail. She had AIDS. It was 1985, and America as a society was terrified of the disease. Rumors flew of people contracting HIV, the virus that led to AIDS, from toilet seats, handshakes, and door handles.

It was a time of fear, and Chuck Colson was not immune to it. Could he be risking his life by this momentary visit?

Where other chaplains and visitors had refused to go to Bessie, however, he ventured ahead, feeling "absolute terror," as he later recalled. When he reached Bessie's cell, he thought about a television clip of Mother Teresa, the diminutive nun hugging AIDS victims without hesitation or personal concern. Replaying that moment in his mind, he went into Bessie's cell. It was small and dark, and Bessie was not well.

Colson spoke calmly with the dying woman, getting to know her briefly. Then he turned the conversation to spiritual matters:

> After chatting a few minutes, I came right to the point. "Bessie," I said, "Do you know the Lord?"
>
> "I want to," she replied softly. "But I don't always feel like He's there." And her voice trailed off.
>
> "Would you like to pray with me to know Christ as your Savior?" I asked.
>
> Bessie looked down, twisted a Kleenex in her thin hands, and finally whispered, "Yes, I would."[2]

Bessie then prayed to receive Christ as her Savior. It was a simple prayer in an isolated wing of a North Carolina prison. No cameras were present; no confetti poured from the ceiling. Colson had only a few minutes with the suffering woman, but he made them count.

Before he left, he warmly embraced Bessie. It was a moment that symbolized the post-conversion narrative of Colson's life: going into hard places to preach the gospel so that captives, lost and without hope just as he once was, might be freed.

Long before Colson ministered to prisoners, he found himself facing the very real prospect of becoming one. In June 1974, he was standing before a judge in a federal courtroom in Washington, DC. Colson was in the hands of the law. On June 21, 1974, Judge Gerhard Gesell would hand down his sentence.

Colson hoped and even expected when he entered the courtroom that fateful morning that he would be able to avoid going to jail. He was shocked when Gesell sentenced him to one to three years in prison and a fine of five thousand dollars.[3] His family was devastated. Months of prayers for release had not resulted in the end they desired. Colson was convicted of a felony. Colson's verdict entered him into a category that, in the eyes of some onlookers, would forever define him: guilty.

At forty-three years of age, Colson's winning streak had ended. The man with an impeccable pedigree had crashed to earth. Numerous other members of the Nixon administration met similarly public fates for their roles in Watergate. No other official, however, had a friend offer to serve his sentence, as Al Quie of the Fellowship, a group of Christian men led by Doug Coe, did. Colson declined his generous offer, knowing that his conviction was his alone. He had been part of a group that had shaken the trust of the American people in the presidency. The nation would never be the same.

As later events make clear, Colson's own life was forever altered. In 1976, Colson was signing copies of his autobiography, *Born Again*, when a wild-eyed young man approached him. Colson knew how to handle tough characters, but this one shook him. "I've been trying to decide if I'm going to kill you tonight," the man said. "If you kill me . . . I'll be with Jesus Christ," Colson replied, praying as he stared back at his would-be assailant.[4] Eventually, the man backed out of the bookstore and went on his way, never to cross paths with Colson again. The experience and others like it showed Colson that his public role had placed him in circumstances beyond his control. Some reacted to him with equanimity and fairness. Others refused to forgive him and even hated him for his deeds.[5]

Facing a prison sentence, Colson entrusted himself to God. On July 8, he entered the detention facility, then a common post-sentencing destination of convicted government workers and members of the Mafia. Two months later, he was transferred to the prison camp at Maxwell Air Base in Montgomery, Alabama. Colson was assigned to Dormitory G and given a number symbolizing his new identity: 23226.[6]

Prison was a shock. Colson was one of 250 prisoners in his dormitory and close to 1,000 in the prison camp overall, a common destination of political convicts (in 2014, Jesse Jackson, Jr., the former US Congressman from Illinois, served time in this facility).[7] Colson's first night was awful. Like many prisoners, Colson frequently woke up, losing needed rest. The nights blended into one another, leaving him perpetually discouraged.

In his daytime hours, Colson worked menial jobs, doing laundry and cleaning floors. He could have requested better jobs, but he decided against it, knowing that if he sought out special treatment from officials, he would surely receive special treatment of a different kind from inmates. During his seven months in prison, Colson put his head down, followed the rules, and focused on cultivating what Christian brotherhood he could. He attended services led by local Southern Baptist pastor Edmon

Blow, a shouting preacher known widely among the prisoners as "Brother Blow."[8] Brother Blow's only brush with fame was his ministry to Colson, but he played a vital role in the prisoner's life, breathing fresh encouragement into him.

Others Colson encountered in Maxwell ran the spectrum from the formerly famous to the salt of the earth. Colson poured detergent and folded sheets in the laundry facilities alongside a former obstetrician who was once head of the American Medical Association.[9] The man worked calmly, but not all inmates were so disposed. One prisoner in Colson's ward was named Rodriguez. A chain-smoker who suffered numerous seizures during his brief time at Maxwell, Rodriguez was known for causing conflict. As Colson watched, Rodriguez began a fight with a tough inmate who punched Rodriguez to the floor, who was then taken to isolation. Bleeding from his ear, weeping in pain, Rodriguez cried out repeatedly for help. None came. Colson knew that he was in agony but could do nothing to help him. Several hours after the fight, Rodriguez was transferred to another prison. All that was left of his presence were "a few blood stains on the tile floor." Though Colson tried to locate him afterward, he never heard of him again.[10]

This tragic case was emblematic of Colson's time at Maxwell and Holabird. He was able to start Bible studies with fellow prisoners John Corbin and Paul Kramer. He was faithful as a gospel witness and as involved as he could be in helping other inmates.[11] But he was severely limited in his incarceration and could do little to help the struggling, angry men all around him. Colson's sense of compassion was awakened in prison. Being unable to aid others during his sentence left him with a lifelong thirst to help the needy. It was during the period in which he lost his own dignity that his desire to promote the dignity of others roared to life.

Colson's experience in this season is instructive for Christians. Prison was not an easy burden for Colson. When we encounter setbacks as Colson did, and when we face hostility because of the truth, we need to remember that God has not promised us ease and comfort in this world. He has gone way beyond that: he has given us eternal life, and even now we taste it. Our lives are hidden with Christ, bound up with him, and secured for all the ages to come.

When our lives hit a snag, we need to keep trusting God. We don't only follow him when the going is good. We persevere. We pray for grace and strength to face our trials. We never accuse God or blame him for our difficulties, for he gives us trials to grow our faith (James 1). In this way, we avoid what we could call "prosperity lite" theology. In contrast to that wrong teaching, we must remember that Christianity is rugged. It is made for trials. Many religions and worldviews fit with a prosperous way of life. Many of them make us feel good when times are good. But only gospel faith enables us to handle the storms and setbacks that visit us all.

Chuck Colson learned this during his prison sentence. This was a very challenging time for him. His father died, his family encountered legal trouble, and just days before he was released, the Virginia Supreme Court disbarred him. In late January 1975, however, months before he reached the minimum part of his one-to-three year sentence, Judge Gesell released Colson. Joyfully received by Patty and his children, Colson headed home, planning a return to law in his home state of Massachusetts. He told Patty first, though, that they needed some time for peace, quiet, and refreshment. "Life will be different for us from now on," he said to her. "No more harassments because I'm no longer a public figure."[12] Listening to her husband, Patty knew he meant what he said. She trusted him. But she could not possibly know just how wrong he was.

Colson's battle with sleep continued after he returned to his home. He found his bed strange and too soft. Prison had hardened him. When he finally fell asleep his first night back, he found himself back in his old prison dormitory, sitting and reading. A grizzled con spoke to him.

> "Hey, Colson, you'll be out of here soon. What are you going to do for us?"
>
> "I'll help in some way," Colson stammered, conscious of many gazes directed his way. "I'll never forget this stinking place or you guys."
>
> "They all say that," replied Archie. "I've seen you big shots come and go. They all say the same thing. Then they get out and forget us fast. Ain't nobody cares about us. Nobody."
>
> "I'll remember, Archie," said Colson.
>
> "Bull!" Archie shouted.[13]

Colson awoke from this exchange—which was a replay of an actual conversation he had behind bars—shaken and haunted. He had left prison, but prison, it seemed, had not left him.

Colson's adjustment to the outside world took time. His brothers in the Fellowship came alongside him as he transitioned. The group was unusual, composed of political types who took the rare step of crossing partisan lines to meet together for prayer, encouragement, and instruction. Doug Coe led the

Fellowship, and US Senator Harold Hughes, Jr., Minnesota Congressman Al Quie, and Texas judge Graham Purcell made up the core.[14] Colson had drawn strength and direction from the group during his pre-prison days. Upon his release, the Fellowship hoped that Colson would commence working for it on different projects involving speaking and Christian advocacy. The idea of some kind of ministry appealed to him, but Colson was developing his own vision for the present: he wanted to write a book about his conversion.

Colson had a major opportunity on this front. Books on Watergate were bestsellers in the mid-70s, and few people in the world had been closer to the center of power—and corruption— than Colson. If he wanted, he could make a mint telling stories, dishing dirt, and clearing his name. This was not an unusual path to take for a former official like Colson. Though he had taken his lumps, Colson still had options, even lucrative ones.

He did not seize them. Instead of writing a personal tell-all, he decided to focus on his conversion story. He earned a small advance from Chosen Books, a small publisher in pastoral Virginia. Despite its humble start, Chosen struck big with the publication of Corrie ten Boom's *The Hiding Place*, an engrossing chronicle of the Dutchwoman's participation in hiding Jews from their Nazi pursuers in World War II. With books like this and David Wilkerson's *The Cross and the Switchblade*, the press cultivated a reputation for telling powerful stories of spiritual triumph in desperate circumstances.[15] Colson's story fit this profile. In 1974, Patty gave Chuck the name for his book, pointing out the phrase "born again" in a Catholic hymnal.[16] Colson immediately liked the title. He went to work dictating, writing, and editing it.

As he labored over the book, Colson stewed on his desire to get involved with prison work. He did not know how to begin, but found a kindred soul in Harold Hughes, himself a former prisoner. The two paid a visit to the head of the federal Bureau of Prisons, Norman Carlson. Drawing from his own recent background, Colson shared his opinion with Carlson that prisons generally failed to rehabilitate their inmates. They were effective at keeping them in; they were not effective at sending them out, enabling them to become contributing members of society.

Colson spoke straightforwardly of the need of every prisoner—and every person—for Jesus Christ. He alone could "heal and reconcile" the wounded and weak. Carlson listened patiently and impassively, asked some questions, and then said simply, "Go ahead with your plans, Mr. Colson, Senator Hughes."[17]

Colson almost fell out of his chair. He had just been granted access to go into any federal prison in the country and choose inmates for spiritual training. This development did not obscure the fact that Colson and Hughes had little idea of what ministry to prisoners should entail. Undeterred by their lack of experience, they began forming plans for their ministry. They started small, bringing twelve convicts together for spiritual training.

At the first gathering, held in a mission in Arlington, Virginia, in early November 1975, Hughes stood up and grabbed the attention of the prisoners. He made no bones about the nature of the fledgling program the prisoners had entered, telling them they were in Arlington "to learn what it means to be disciples who deny everything else in the world for the sake of Jesus Christ." The former senator with the booming voice had no trouble getting the interest of his hearers. "I was thrown in jail in six states when I was an alcoholic," he said, "and should have been in 20. Chuck has been there too. So we're no better than you, but we are going to teach you."[18]

It was an attention-getting start from an attention-getting man. From tiny Ida Grove, Iowa, Hughes served his country in World War II and became known as a hard drinker. Following the war, his life spiraled downward as he regularly drank himself into a stupor. In his autobiography, he recounted one drunken interaction with his mother that shocked him. He came home from a round of drinking, and she smelled whiskey on his breath. Her request that he stop his habit only riled him up:

> I rushed into our bedroom, rummaged behind the shoes in the closet, pulled out a fifth of whisky, stamped back into the kitchen, and slammed the bottle down on the table so hard it foamed. "By God," I yelled, "I'll drink wherever I want to: I'm a man now, fought through a war for my country, and am sick of being treated like a kid!"

His mother did not respond, but looked at him in terror, afraid for her life and her son.[19]

Tall, powerful, and handsome, Hughes lived like a pugilistic James Dean. He fought authority at both a psychological and physical level. Once, when a town sheriff sought his arrest, Hughes beat him up, leaving him in the dust while he fled.[20] One night in 1954, Hughes drank himself into a stupor. He had broken a promise to his wife, Eva, coming home hours after he was due. This was a common occurrence. He stumbled into his house, riddled with guilt. "I found myself wandering about the house, a sense of blackness closing in on me," he remembered in his autobiography. He came upon his 12-gauge Remington shotgun, sat down in his bathtub, and put his finger on the trigger. His life nearly at an end, Hughes began sobbing and cried out to God: "Oh God, I'm a failure, a drunk, a liar, and a cheat. I'm lost and hopeless and want to die. Forgive me for doing this," he cried out, sliding into the tub.

That simple prayer changed his life. As he sobbed to himself in his tub, "a strange peace gently settled" over him. In that moment, despite all his rage and rancor, he experienced forgiveness: "My sins seemed to evaporate like moisture spots under a hot, bright sun." He was now conscious of the Lord and his goodness. "God was reaching down and touching me. A God Who cared, a God Who loved me, Who was concerned for me despite my sins." Weeping on his bathroom floor, Hughes reached the end of himself. "I gave Him myself totally. 'Whatever You ask me to do, Father,' I cried through hot tears, 'I will do it.'"[21]

Harold Hughes had found true peace. He soon began spending time with his wife and daughters and started listening to messages by Billy Graham. The evangelist impressed him "by his straight-on-for-Jesus stance." Hughes even started teaching Sunday school.[22] His transformation was remarkable. He made a decision to enter politics in Iowa and soon enjoyed a meteoric rise in the Democratic Party. He worked as a lobbyist until the early 1960s, became the governor of Iowa from 1963 through 1968, and won election as a US Senator in 1968. He flirted with a presidential run in 1971, but decided to devote himself to serving the Lord through prison ministry, anti-drug campaigns, and other spiritual work.

No one would have put Colson and Hughes together as ministry co-laborers. They had engaged in direct political combat over the years, each of them outspoken for his party. Initially, Hughes was uneasy about working with a man he once hated—and who once hated him. Soon after Colson's conversion, Coe arranged a meeting between the men and several others. Colson introduced himself to the group, and Hughes found himself warming to Colson as he described his fledgling faith: "As Colson talked, his voice caught at times and I sensed how difficult it was for him to share his experience, knowing my skepticism. He went on with his story, speaking slowly and self-consciously picking a bit of lint from his slacks."

Colson spoke of his desire "to overcome a lifelong dependency on pride" and to defeat his "arrogance" and "doubts." Hughes later recalled how Colson understood the work of Christ in his life: "It all fitted into place," he said huskily, looking up at me, "when I was able to see Who Jesus was."[23] In this moment, Hughes found his heart softening. Colson needed help and said as much: "I'd be grateful for any help you can give me." His humility won Hughes over from that day forward: "I knew in my heart he had been forgiven through the blood of Jesus, just as I had been forgiven."[24] The two enemies had become friends—and more than friends, brothers.

Colson and Hughes each softened as believers, but neither lost his edge. They were hard-charging leaders who met Jesus on the edge of a knife. Coming to faith had wrecked and ruined their earlier selves. They were remade men, both keenly aware of the transformative nature of divine grace. God had hunted them down. Now they were in search of others just like them, lost and without hope.

The two men recognized that nothing but the gospel was going to help their students. They set out to instruct them in the basics of spiritual life, emphasizing the necessity and power of the cross. The twelve prisoners listening to the two ex-cons did not need life tips. They needed the work of Christ to wash over their hearts. That, and not positive thinking, was their only hope. This program found immediate success. It brought prison ministry to unexpected places. In the second week of the program, for example, Colson and Hughes took the unusual step of bringing the inmates to Capitol Hill, where they made the rounds, visiting senators, the State Department, and other key offices.[25]

The uniqueness of the visit was not lost on various eminent figures. One senator later told Colson that he had been shocked to see prisoners in the Senate offices. He was intrigued, though, and decided to talk and pray with the group. As he listened to the inmates pray, he was startled by the authenticity of their petitions. He did not pray in these tones; his was a more genteel, quiet faith. He went home that very night, he told Colson, and shared with his wife about the prisoners: "I told her that we needed what those inmates had." Colson was encouraged by this point, but his friend was not finished: "So the two of us prayed together that Jesus Christ would come into our lives as He had in theirs."[26] Colson's makeshift tour of the Senate had led to the salvation not of an inmate, but of a US Senator and his wife.

During the next year, Colson brought more than one hundred prisoners to DC. The results of this program were immediate and dramatic. The busy schedule took a toll on Colson. He soon realized that he needed time for deeper reflection on the program's future. This ministry to prisoners needed more formal contours, even as he needed further guidance and clarity of vision. In July 1976, Colson took a vacation with Patty in Oregon. Sitting by the sea, he sketched out some thoughts on a yellow legal pad in an effort to determine the priorities and needs of his spiritual life. Three in particular stand out:

> *Conversion*: For me, an emotional experience which broke my proud resistance and convinced me that Jesus Christ is who He says He is. Such a "crisis" conversion is like suddenly stepping from a dark room into a brightly lighted one but is a long way from learning how to live in the new environment.
>
> *Compassion*: In prison I also first "heard" His words about the "least of these." On the cross, Jesus took on the suffering of all mankind. Are we not to do the same?
>
> *Knowledge*: The awareness of how little I really knew about the Christian faith—an important milestone because it started me digging into books on theology, seeking out good teachers, hungering for understanding. Still, the hard questions throw me.[27]

This memo charts not only where Colson was in 1976, but also where he would go in coming years. When it came to laying down his life for others, he had not "been put to that test," but showed a willingness to embrace it. Colson did not want to play his life safe. He did not desire that God would make his path easy. His animating interest was in service to God. Yet he was not sure what this meant: "How does one serve God?" he wrote at the close of the memo. He did not know, but he was no doubt thinking back on his prison experience, as he constantly did in this period.

Colson may have thought then of Rodriguez, flailing at the world, begging for help one minute, inviting destruction the next. He knew that prison was a deadening place, one that took dignity and hope away from convicts. He also was aware that many prisoners were unlike him. They did not have means; they did not have well-connected friends to assist them; they did not have any hope. Colson also saw that, despite his own trials, he had been given much by God. At this point, however, he did not know where to fully apply his gifts. He would soon find out.

———

A decade after Colson pondered his future in Oregon, he met Bessie Shipp in her cell. By then, Colson's prison ministry had taken form and shape. Prison Fellowship was thriving, with chapters and volunteers and a large budget. At its core, however, the ministry had not changed at all. Colson did with the dying woman what he could not do with Rodriguez. He entered Bessie's cell, took her hand, and told her that though this life was cruel and all too short, eternal life could be hers through repentance and faith in Jesus Christ. In that moment, Bessie prayed with Chuck. She, too, experienced the power of the cross.

When she was released not long after (due in large part to Colson's intervention), Bessie did not return to her criminal ways. She went to her church and testified of her newfound faith in Jesus.[28] By all accounts, her testimony electrified her surroundings. The woman exhibited a joy she had never before possessed.

Bessie's faith buoyed her, but she was not well. She was dying from AIDS. Just weeks after her release, she lay in a hospital bed. Visited by a faithful Christian minister named Al Lawrence, she did not request prayer for healing. She knew she was not long for this world. She told Al, "Don't pray for heaven because heaven is already mine. I have confessed Christ before my brothers and sisters. I am at peace."[29] She continued in halting tones: "There is just one more thing I would like to do on this earth, and that is, I would like to get baptized." A nurse came to her side and asked what she had said, but by then, Bessie was too weak to talk. Just after midnight, connected to numerous tubes and hospital equipment, Bessie was baptized. Hours later, she died.[30]

Bessie's story points us to a driving reality in Colson's life: whether he was talking quietly with Bessie or shaking hands with a senator, he believed in the transformative power of Christ. His fledgling ministry program, unorthodox in its design, achieved unusual results from the outset. It did so because Colson believed in the power of the gospel. Though a young Christian, he knew one essential reality very well: the message of Jesus Christ is no respecter of persons. It does not conform to social conventions and class sympathies. Some of Colson's peers might have wondered if witnessing to senators required a genteel, sophisticated witness. Colson knew, however, that the gospel minded no barriers, social or otherwise. As time would tell, this was the essential conviction of his life's work.

We need to recover Colson's confidence in the gospel and act on it. Our context does not need a specially tailored salvation for modern ears. It needs the simple message of salvation. The gospel saves sinners. This is true if you're a political power broker, and this is true if you've been left behind by society. Christians today are challenged to damp down our confidence in salvation and to accept that people don't really change. Colson's life shows us the opposite is true.

We should take heart from the way God used the early efforts of Colson and Hughes. They did not begin their work among prisoners with elaborate plans. They simply started discipling people, training them in the basics of biblical faith. Many believers today are knocked off-kilter by the strong anti-theistic spirit of our time. We feel as if there is a big bad atheistic wolf waiting to devour us around every corner, and so we hide our light. It is good to be prepared and to be as theologically grounded as we can be. But we also need to get off the couch. The darkness of our world should not stop us from expecting God to show up. God is bigger than any challenge. He loves to bless our acts of faith. He delights to reward not only the mature disciple, but also the young one.

Reading Colson's story, we are reminded of Christ's apostles. They hadn't had seminary training. They were considered simple in the eyes of the learned. But they were unafraid of the world and unashamed of the gospel. They preached it and watched as people were converted. Wherever we're working, whatever vocation God has given us, we need to get active in his name, and not let our doubts or fears stop us from being a witness. We're not all Billy Graham. As Christians, we are all saved, though, and the power of God is in our bones.

Dwelling on these truths can move us beyond our worries. It did for Colson. Soon after he entered Bessie Shipp's cell, he was no longer afraid. Soon after he left it, Bessie was no longer a prisoner.

FOUR

ROOTS

Chuck Colson was spellbound. He was in the presence of Francis Schaeffer, a genuinely brilliant intellect, a "prophet" as he would later describe the man. As they walked and talked in a mountainside village in Switzerland in summer 1977, Colson found himself listening for long spells of time. Like a character in a Greek play, Colson had come to L'Abri in little Huemoz, Switzerland, to learn from the evangelical oracle who dwelt in his high-altitude Swiss chalet.[1]

The two men were a funny pair. Schaeffer's slim five-foot-eight-inch stature, knee-length pants, and flowing beard cut a notable contrast with Colson's lanky six-foot-one-inch build and preppy ensemble. But the two men were a marvelous match in intellect and ability. Both had quick-fire minds that could readily grasp concepts and new ideas. Both were effective leaders able to marshal support for a cause and drive it forward. In later years, both men would be credited for the evangelical worldview renaissance, with its focus on understanding Christianity not as a set of moral behaviors but as a coherent body of explosive teachings. On this day, however, Schaeffer filled the role of teacher and Colson the role of student. For an entire day they talked, and talked, and talked.

Chuck Colson emerged from his time on the mountain with the prophet with fresh vision and purpose. He could no longer just act and decide. He wanted to think and ponder too. After a frenetic and fruitful few years, he saw what his thriving ministry needed most of all: roots.

———

Soon after Colson wrote his ten-point memo to himself in 1976, his work in prisons became a formal ministry under the name Prison Fellowship. Colson and Patty took a trip to the Oregon coast in the summer of 1976. Staying at the beautiful beach home of Oregon senator Mark Hatfield, Colson and his wife talked over their future hopes.[2] Colson had been both catalyzed by prison ministry and confused by it. Surely he should choose a more obvious path—business, consulting, law?

When it came time to talk with Patty, he was shocked when she expressed the opinion that they should embrace his gospel work. In words that elegantly expressed Patty's supportive, giving nature, she told her conflicted husband that, contrary to her desire for a quiet life, she recognized that God had other plans. "Christ," she told Chuck, "really does make all the difference," indicating that her walk with the Lord was now a deeply personal one.[3] But that wasn't all. "I see now that God wants you to be in full-time ministry. We can't deny that and we shouldn't, no matter what our preferences might be . . . if that's what you want, I'm with you all the way."[4] These simple words moved

Colson to his core. They signaled to him that his wife was by his side, no matter what, come what may. Her support made all the difference.

"So where do we go next, Chuck Colson?" Patty said.

"Into the prisons, honey—into every prison in this country," Chuck responded.

"They will never be the same if you do," Patty predicted.

"I pray to God that you're right—that He will see to it that they never are the same again," said Chuck.[5]

Prison Fellowship was incorporated a few weeks later on August 10, 1976.

The budget for the ministry in its first few years was a shadow of what it would become: $85,000 in 1976 and $440,000 in 1977, but these numbers are misleading.[6] At this time, Colson was the major supporter of the organization. For the rest of his life, the ministry executive faced allegations that his turn to ministry was a counterfeit, and that he had simply switched vocational tracks to make money off gullible Christian people. In reality, Colson donated 90 percent of his income to Prison Fellowship, a typically bold amount from a man of principle.[7] Though he wore Brooks Brothers, his employees noted that he rarely purchased new clothes, preferring to wear out his familiar ones.[8] Colson had a taste for the good life, but his conversion refocused his interests.

Colson focused in these early years on establishing new chapters of Prison Fellowship. According to Jonathan Aitken, the ministry stretched across the country by 1979. Nearly ten thousand inmates participated in training seminars staged by a constellation of professional staff and volunteers working in concert with prison chaplains.[9] In this early phase of Prison Fellowship, the typical format involved teaching in a local prison for a set period of time.

There was little fluff to the ministry. Colson and his team visited prisons to communicate the essential truths of Christianity. They opened the Scripture, explained its doctrines, and called their hearers to repentance and faith. Colson had a direct, forceful style that translated well to the prison setting. He was not yet the polished speaker that he would become, but he was honing his craft and winning a hearing everywhere he went.

Though Colson's message was straightforward, his operation was sophisticated. Few prison ministers, after all, had more administrative experience than the former White House official. He needed such acumen. As Colson's popularity surged in the late 1970s and early 1980s, he received an unending stream of requests. From the early days of Prison Fellowship until Colson's waning years, the founder sought to accommodate everyone he could. This meant operating on a minute-by-minute schedule that left little time for freelancing. The day's itinerary would have boggled a calmer man: meet with a governor and his cabinet; counsel a weeping inmate on death row; speak in chapel to one hundred prisoners; talk in snatches with chaplains; meet with volunteers and staff to discuss improvement of operations and procedures.

Everything Chuck Colson did became big. He had a native talent for entrepreneurship and organizational cultivation. With his fierce will, his restless intelligence, and his desire to get the gospel out, Colson could not help but lend strength to any initiative he undertook. His was not a lonely revolution, either. A consummate leader, Colson inspired scores of people around him, opening their eyes to opportunities and needs they had not previously considered. To be sure, Christian chaplains had brought the gospel to prisoners since prisons existed.[10] But Chuck Colson, buoyed by a sense of divine purpose, elevated prison ministry to new heights in America and abroad in the years that followed.

It is easy to forget how common imprisonment is in the Bible. From nearly the start to the finish, those who follow God have a remarkable habit of ending up in jail. There is often a direct connection between obedience to God and incarceration. Joseph resisted the advances of an adulterous woman and found himself in prison for two years. Daniel and his friends were jailed because they refused to stop worshipping their God. John the Baptist spent time in prison before being beheaded for publicly decrying sin. Jesus was a captive before he was crucified. The apostle Paul wrote "prison letters," rejoicing in the fact that "what has happened to me has really served to advance the gospel," as he told the Philippian church (Phil. 1:12).

There is something remarkable in this thread. We cannot miss how it runs counter to our common expectations as believers. When trials come, we often despair or grow angry with God. We feel as if God has betrayed us and given us an unusually subpar Christian experience. But God never promises us earthly prosperity. We might think we deserve it, and he is often generous to bless us beyond belief. But he regularly calls his people to suffer hardship in order to testify to his greatness. We dream of a penthouse, but God may well give us a prison cell.

Chuck Colson was given eyes to see this biblical truth. He might have seemed strange among fellow Ivy League graduates, but compared to the span of faithful Christians in Scripture and in church history, he was no anomaly. His experience enabled him to minister grace to people and to build an organization that ensured that the prisoners of America would not be forgotten.

During the 1980s, Colson bolstered the program of Prison Fellowship. The ministry transitioned from an in-prison training program drawing a few hundred prisoners at a time to an international outfit composed of numerous major projects, each with its own staff. The organization went from a horizontal model to a vertical one. Prison Fellowship would always conduct biblical training as its core work, but as Colson considered new prospects, the ministry added distinct projects that catalyzed its influence. After Colson visited the Walla Walla prison in Washington state, reputedly the worst prison in America, he launched Justice Fellowship in 1983.[11] The department focused on prison justice, on improving the experience of prisoners.

Justice Fellowship was in some sense the ideas lab of Prison Fellowship. It allowed Colson not only to teach spiritual truth but also to advocate for system reform. Colson's political beliefs always ran red; he never wavered from his political conservatism. But on the issue of the living conditions of inmates, Colson found himself at odds with a range of peers throughout his career. He often heard of the inhumanity of criminals, and he never ceased to bristle at it. The major reason for this divergence of opinion, of course, was his personal experience.

Prison for Colson was personal. Unlike many citizens, he could not conceive of it in the abstract. He had eaten the awful food. He had smelled the soiled air. He had heard the screams of men tortured, night after night, by nightmares that were no imagined drama but a rehearsal of everyday life. He did not disagree in the least with the belief that prisoners were sinners, corrupted and broken by their sin. But as a man of conscience and compassion, Colson also knew that every prisoner was a human being made in the image of God, invested with dignity, no matter what he or she had done. Because of this belief, he never failed to see the potential in any person.

This is instructive for us. If we want to minister grace to people, we can only gain perspective by entering into their situations. This will challenge us. If we have nice lives, we will not find it easy to go into hard places. But doing so awakens us to the challenges before us.

I came to see this firsthand a few years ago. I have always been passionately pro-life. In high school I wrote an essay for the *Downeast Coastal Press*, my county's local paper, decrying abortion. In college I had conversations with friends who did not share my convictions. This was fairly standard pro-life involvement. But my involvement stopped there.

After all, there was little I could do to reverse *Roe v. Wade*. Plus, I didn't feel prepared or situated to be the kind of pro-life advocate who popped up in NBC News clips, holding a sign and being arrested outside of a judicial building. So for years I was pro-life. But I wasn't *that* pro-life. I didn't see any way this situation could or would change. Save for the miraculous and direct intervention of God, abortion felt so big and distant and cruelly inevitable.

In 2012, I came into contact with a ministry called Speak for the Unborn.[12] The work was simple: area Christians went to the Louisville abortion clinic and sought to share the gospel and winsomely encourage women to save their children. I was thankful to hear about this ministry, but I didn't think much more about it. Then, one day it hit me: I could go down to Market Street. I could join this work. So I went. It was not easy. I was kicked, sworn at, and threatened physically by the pro-choice "escorts" who encourage women to kill their babies. But it was worth it all.

My formerly disengaged stance is common in the church. Too many of us pray and then lift our heads, looking around to see whom God will tap to go and suffer. Anyone but us. But the Bible's teaching on being "salt and light" is not intended for the easy places of the world. It is intended for the hard places, and it is we who are called to love our neighbors as ourselves and to do good to all men (Matt. 5:13–16; 22:39; Gal. 6:10). This will mean embracing discomfort, even hardship. As we embrace suffering, we will see flashes of divine grace.

One cold morning, some church members and I were able to talk with a young couple who were walking hurriedly toward the abortion clinic. On that cold morning, a miracle happened. The couple left the clinic. She was weeping. He was smiling. They went into the crisis pregnancy center nearby. They received some information and counseling. Months later, the young woman gave birth to a beautiful little girl. I got to meet the couple and talk with them after her birth. Writing this even now, I get chills, as I do every time I think about God's kindness to this couple and their decision to save their baby's life.[13]

God loves to bless even the halting efforts of his people. Ministry in Christ's name is never going to be easy or enduringly popular. Jesus was hated, and we will be hated (John 17:1–8). But in working in his name, we can experience something better than popularity. We can suffer with Christ, and go outside the safe confines of the city gate, and watch as God works in our world to overcome sin (Heb. 13:12). This was part of Chuck

Colson's makeup. He loved the challenge of prison ministry. He loved to have the odds against him, to feel the winds of culture in his face. He was galvanized by risk.

Colson knew early on as a Christian just how enjoyable serving the Lord was. But he also knew that his grasp of Scripture was limited. He wanted to keep ministering grace to the needy, but he needed a stronger spiritual foundation. Michael Cromartie, a young, book-loving staffer helped him greatly in this respect. Cromartie, now vice president of the Ethics and Public Policy Center in Washington DC, came to Colson's staff after graduating from Covenant College in Lookout Mountain, Georgia.[14] He assisted Colson in the late 1970s with his research and writing.

Cromartie was an excellent complement to Colson, if an unexpected one. The bearded young researcher was contemplative and grounded in historical theology; the veteran executive was hard driving and in search of deeper theological roots. Cromartie later remembered his boss as a workaholic and a "speeding train going down the rails."[15] From his early days at Prison Fellowship, he saw his role as throwing "heavy cargo" in front of the locomotive. Colson would not allow himself the time to enter a degree program at one of the respected evangelical seminaries—Trinity Evangelical Divinity School or Gordon-Conwell Theological Seminary. Cromartie knew this. He also knew, however, that he could aid Colson's theological formation in an on-the-fly fashion.

In the late 70s Cromartie began arranging meetings between Colson and Christian scholars. "I could just phone them up," he later said, "because everybody wanted to meet Chuck."[16] The professors of evangelicalism's top schools were intrigued by the opportunity to meet one of the most famous public figures in

America. Cromartie noted that Protestant historian Martin Marty, for example, once met Colson at a Chicago airport. The two talked for several hours about "American religious history." Cromartie encouraged Colson not to give up on any political connections in this phase of his life, when Colson was understandably disillusioned by his past career.

Colson loved much of what Cromartie recommended. "I introduced him to [Abraham] Kuyper, Wilberforce, the reformed world-and-life view," Cromartie reflected, and Colson was off to the races. In this tradition, Colson found the theological orientation he craved. According to Cromartie, this general view was "Augustinian," grounded in the conviction trumpeted by the fifth-century bishop of Hippo that Christians, residents of the "city of God," must also be responsible citizens of the "city of man," the fallen world.[17] Cromartie's memos on these leading lights helped convince Colson that he yet had a role to play in the public square.

Cromartie's encouragement launched Colson into a lifelong self-education project. Colson hungered to learn more and identified a range of thinkers and leaders whose writings and deeds could instruct him. Looking back at the figures Colson regularly cited, names like Kuyper, Wilberforce, theologian R. C. Sproul, theologian Carl Henry, and apologist Francis Schaeffer emerge as his major pedagogues. There were numerous other influences—C. S. Lewis, John Calvin, Martin Luther, John Wesley, Jonathan Edwards, and others—but these five stand out for their formative role in Colson's early theological development. In what follows, we will briefly trace the effect of each of these five Christians on Colson.

ABRAHAM KUYPER

Abraham Kuyper was born to an aristocratic family in the Netherlands in 1837. Like Colson, Kuyper filled many roles in his long and impressive career. He was a local church pastor, the founder and chief voice of two newspapers, the leader of the Christian Democrats (a Dutch political party he founded), the author of more than two dozen books, and the prime minister of the Netherlands from 1901 to 1905.

Like Colson, Kuyper relished work in two worlds—politics and ministry. Kuyper started out in ministry and moved into politics (Colson did the reverse). Kuyper believed that Christ claimed all of life. His famous dictum, "There is not one square inch of the cosmos over which Christ does not cry, 'Mine!'" reflected his belief that Christians could serve the Lord in any vocation, whether country preacher, attentive mother, or newspaper columnist.[18]

Perhaps most important, Kuyper's life backed up his talk. He not only served as prime minister, but he invested in the future of his country by founding the Free University of Amsterdam, a school intended to train the next generation of Christian leaders—whether pastors, theologians, politicians, or economists. The school no longer has the strong Reformed bent of its early years, but it continues to rank as one of the top two hundred universities in the world nearly 140 years after its founding.

As is apparent in this brief survey of Kuyper's program, he had more energy than one career could contain. Abraham Kuyper took God at his Word. If God was sovereign, as Scripture indicated he was, then his people were free to give him glory by laboring in his name, conscious of the Lord's ability to accomplish whatever he desired.

Divine sovereignty was not a hindrance to human agency in Kuyper's mind. It was a spark, a blast of nitro that could fuel many daring initiatives that other Christians—less conscious of the freeing greatness of God—would not feel free to attempt. The effort might fail, or it might succeed in unprecedented fashion. Either way, the believer was called to dream big and then get to work.

Kuyper offered Colson the ultimate incentive to action, for here was a man who didn't simply publish a grand strategy but lived it. He was—like Colson—as good in the backrooms where decisions were made as he was out front, promoting the strategy to thousands of startled onlookers. In Kuyper's vision of unimpeded cultural influence and his tireless work to invest in his country, Colson found inspiration for his own work. A believer could not only preach the gospel but also reform a society. This was the fuel Colson was looking for.

WILLIAM WILBERFORCE

The second figure to leave a mark on Colson was William Wilberforce, the longtime member of British Parliament (1780–1825). Wilberforce was for Colson an example of public courage, of faith unleashed in the public square. The cosmopolitan evangelical took on the single most noxious element of British society, the slave trade, and during the course of his five-decade career vanquished it. Wilberforce was an activist driven by principle. This appealed at an existential level to Colson; this was who Colson was.

Because of his conviction that slavery was wrong—a conviction grounded in Christian theology—Wilberforce agitated and spoke and voted to outlaw the slave trade. The elegant sophisticate, trained in the *politesse* of high English society, knew how to roll up his sleeves and make things happen. "Almighty God has set before me two great objectives," he wrote in 1787, "the abolition of the slave trade and the reformation of manners."[19] Wilberforce could not content himself with proclamation; he had to get active, and he did. He tapped his network, called the Clapham Sect, and went to work with fellow elites like William Pitt and Granville Sharp to form, advocate for, and pass the legislation that would erode, bill by bill, the slave trade.

Wilberforce championed his cause while moving in the circles of influence that made Britain go. He ate sumptuous multicourse meals, attended balls and other functions, and performed the elaborate, formal courtesies of the pre-Victorian world. But all his glad-handing was driven by a conscience that burned with a hatred of evil and injustice. This was an early *Downton Abbey*—but with an abolitionist Parliamentarian stalking the hallowed country estate.

As Colson read about Wilberforce, he discovered that theologian John Wesley had impelled the young politician to oppose slavery. In later years, Colson frequently quoted Wesley's parting charge to Wilberforce:

> Unless the Divine Power has raised you up to be as Athanasius, *contra mundum*, I see not how you can go through your glorious enterprise in opposing that execrable villainy which is the scandal of religion, of England, and of human nature. Unless God has raised you up for this very thing, you will

be worn out by the opposition of men and devils, but if God be for you, who can be against you? Are all of them together stronger than God? Oh, be not weary in well doing. Go on, in the name of God and in the power of His might, till even American slavery, the vilest that ever saw the sun, shall vanish away before it.[20]

Behind Wesley's plea to Wilberforce was unshakeable confidence in the Almighty. Wesley's words reinforced Colson's view that he must be prepared to stand *contra mundum*, "against the world," in his own quest to advance justice and oppose evil.

As he studied, Colson was mapping in his mind his own great objectives: the wide-scale preaching of the gospel in prisons and the reform of the corrupted American mind and culture. It took some time for these great ambitions to fully flower, but in time, they would. Colson was coming to understand that there is no tension between preaching the gospel and practicing the faith. Too often, Christians treat the gospel and ethics as if they are separate matters. Some believers like preaching the word of Christ; some like thinking about traditional ethical topics. There doesn't seem to be much connection between the two.

In reality, the gospel creates ethics. When Jesus saves you, you emerge from the experience a new person with a new set of priorities and beliefs. You can no longer treat life lightly (Ps. 139). You are given a great love for the natural family, which owes to God's intelligent design (Gen. 2:14–25). You seek to advocate for religious freedom because you recognize that without it, people will wither and suffer (Matt. 22:21).

The gospel creates ethics. It brings to life our best instincts. The message of Christ creates in the redeemed a thirst for racial unity (Eph. 2:15). It overcomes tension between the sexes (Gal. 3:27–28). It removes barriers between social classes (Philem. 1:16). It gives us a hunger to work and a zest for creativity (Col. 3:23). It makes us weep for every human person, made in the image of God, who suffers under the curse, and it causes us to want to do good to everyone (Gal. 6:10). It awakens us to the duties of citizenship and the need to pray for political righteousness (Rom. 13; 1 Tim. 2:2). In sum, the gospel causes us to want to be salt and light in a darkened world in every possible way (Matt. 5:13–16).

Faith in Christ bestows on us a convictional inheritance. We don't fashion our own understanding of righteousness, justice, fairness, and mercy as believers. There's no fast-food ethical menu that allows us to ignore certain dimensions of equity. Though some issues loom larger than others, we recognize that our ethics and convictions are not ultimately our own. They are God's. We are *given* these insights by his Word. Standing for biblical truths and Christian morality is not a problem for us to solve. We have an ethical inheritance to steward.

We must also note that our ethics are our apologetics. This is not to sideline questions of the canon of Scripture, of the nature of knowledge, or of the existence of God. We can and should address these matters with the help of professional apologists. But we note as well that we live in an era much like the first century. Our belief in human dignity, in the call to seek the good of our neighbor, and our desire to live a holy life will speak a powerful word to our non-Christian friends. As they see us living virtuously, exhibiting genuine care for the weak and the suffering, they will witness a living body of apologetics. They will discover a way of life that commends the faith to the point of being evangelistic. Ethics and moral convictions are not for discussion forums and classroom debates. They are made for the rough-and-tumble of life, and they will prove attractive and even winning to those given eyes to see the beauty of holiness-made-flesh.

This frees us as God's people. It reminds us that there is no hostility between private Christianity and public Christianity. Ethics and moral convictions do not get in the way of gospel preaching. The gospel creates holiness in sinful people; ethics, moral convictions, and righteous actions are nothing other than holiness in practice. We don't choose whether we want to be an evangelistic Christian or a moral Christian. The same gospel that saves our wicked hearts makes us want to live out our faith in our everyday world. Our great God is holy, and we want to be holy. By his power, we are.

William Wilberforce had just this longing. He is one of historic Christianity's prime examples of the power of a vivified conscience. He did not work alone, however. Wesley, John Newton, and the relatively unknown pastor John Venn all preached in such a manner to stir Wilberforce to action.[21] He regularly borrowed Venn's sermons to guide his thinking on political matters. None of the preachers who influenced Wilberforce shrank back from addressing ethical issues in their sermons. From 1792 to 1813, Venn was the rector of Clapham, a posh area that some would have feared offending. But Venn was fearless. As a result, he put steel in Wilberforce's spine. There was a direct connection between the doctrines of the Scripture and the policies of the young Parliamentarian.

In our day, we must recover this connection. Pastors should not be political, in the sense that they preach in an expository manner about the local ballot initiative rather than biblical books. They should speak with care to specific causes, remaining ever aware of the temptation to politicize the pulpit, a grave mistake. But pastors should be ethical and convictional. They should inform the ethical convictions of their people. They should speak to the major issues of life and of contemporary culture through a thoroughly biblical lens. Pastors are appointed by God to lead in the great project of "mind renewal" (Rom. 12:1–2). They must not leave this work to others. The Bible is authoritative not only for our quiet times but for our public witness.

Christians who exercise their conscience in public become public-square witnesses. The distinction between "public" and "private" Christianity is tenuous in such cases. Not all Christians are called to be political in the sense that they devote their days to campaigns. But all Christians are called to live out their faith and act on their beliefs in public. Anytime we speak up on behalf of the suffering, our witness is public. Anytime we reach out to the needy, our witness is public. Anytime we vote, our witness is public. Unless we purposefully retreat from the world, it is hard to keep our faith private.

We should avoid politicized Christianity. We should feel no guilt, though, over public Christianity. The heroes of Scripture seem, more often than not, to be called to profess their faith and their ethics in public. On this point, the church has underplayed the accounts of figures like Joseph, Moses, Deborah, David, Esther, and Daniel, all of whom were called by God into public confrontation with political powers. This holds equally true in the New Testament. John the Baptist denounced Herod's sexual sin (Matt. 14); Jesus was called before Pilate (John 18); the apostle Paul appealed for justice when captured on the basis of his Roman citizenship (Acts 22).

Above all, we recall that Jesus was crucified in public. He was offered as a spectacle. His gruesome death was an act of shaming, a rebuke to those who would follow his silly cult. But divine irony prevailed. Jesus' public death did not truly signal his shaming and Satan's triumph. It signaled his triumph and Satan's shaming (Col. 2:15). On the cross, Jesus took the sin of his people, becoming a curse for them. Satan's power was broken by Jesus' death.

Before a jeering crowd, a defeated church, and a watching cosmos, Jesus fulfilled the promise made in the garden of Eden. He crushed the head of Satan, and he did so publicly. His kingship was fully realized, and his reign truly began, when he yielded to death. Soon after, he publicly rose to life, appearing to many witnesses. Jesus is no privatized Savior. His death and resurrection signal that he has claimed all the world for his own (Eph. 1).

The church has the joyful duty of making this victory known. We work to advance this spiritual kingdom in the hearts of mankind. This means that we are not allowed to sit out the momentous public-square issues and cultural struggles of our day. Christians in Scripture did not have the luxury of allowing injustice to prevail. They spoke against it. So must we. But this work will require pastors who shape our moral imagination. If the church is weak on ethics and cultural engagement, it is because the pulpit is weak. In our day we can hope and pray that God will strengthen his shepherds, and in turn strengthen the sheep.

The pastor should be the theological guide of his church.[22] He should be the ethical activator of the body, the conscience awakener of the congregation. He will not possess mastery of every issue in the culture. He will, however, preach the whole counsel of the Word, which is shot through with theologically fueled ethics. At base, because God is holy, we hate unholiness in our world and we love righteousness. Everyday believers will only stand for the good, however, when we hear the manifold wisdom of the Bible proclaimed in all its glory from the pulpit.

R. C. SPROUL

Colson encountered the doctrine of God's glory in a powerful way from his third tutor, R. C. Sproul. The son of a blue-collar Pittsburgh worker, Sproul was converted in college and studied for his doctorate at Kuyper's Free University before becoming a professor and pastor in Pennsylvania. As he preached staunch theology in a folksy manner, Sproul acquired a large following. This being the age of Schaeffer, Sproul was asked to start a study center modeled after L'Abri, an initiative that in 1971 became the Ligonier Valley Study Center of Western Pennsylvania. The ministry moved to Orlando in 1984, and Sproul kept up a busy schedule writing numerous books, teaching at schools like Reformed Theological Seminary, and speaking at his Ligonier Ministries conferences to thousands of Christians with a hunger for theology.[23]

When he encountered Sproul's teaching, Colson was experiencing what he later called "spiritual dryness." Cromartie recommended Colson watch the video lectures of Sproul's *The Holiness of God*, and the rest is history:

All I knew about Sproul was that he was a theologian, so I wasn't enthusiastic. After all, I reasoned, theology was for people who had time to study, locked in ivory towers far from the battlefields of human need. However, at my friend's urging I finally agreed to watch Sproul's series.

By the end of the sixth lecture I was on my knees, deep in prayer, in awe of God's absolute holiness. It was a life-changing experience as I gained a completely new understanding of the holy God I believe in and worship . . . this taste of the majesty of God only made me thirst for more of him.[24]

Colson thought that thinking about God in a sustained way belonged to the "ivory tower" and the "study." Theology, as Colson understood it, was for specialists, people who liked to ponder abstract questions that had little to do with real life. Everything changed when Colson popped in Sproul's videotape. He found himself transfixed by the vision of a high and holy God who reigned over all things and ordered all things according to the counsel of his holy will. Like the young monk Martin Luther, whom Sproul discussed in his book and videos, Colson found himself captivated, not put off, by the greatness of God.

Colson emerged from his encounter with Sproul's God-centered teaching with a desire to love God. He found himself deeply grateful to the Lord for "God's love for humanity and how He showed that love by the sacrifice of His Son on the cross."[25] He wanted to know this loving God better, having recognized that God owed him nothing but had chosen to set his grace upon him. Previously, Colson's busy itinerary left him little time to enjoy genuine fellowship with God. After discovering that God's greatness was profoundly practical, sweeping the Christian up in the delight of true knowledge, Colson was driven to make greater time to study the Bible. He knew that he met God there, and he craved further closeness with his Savior and Lord. He was already converted, but under Sproul he was won over to the importance of a theological life.

CARL F. H. HENRY

Sproul laid a sturdy theological foundation for Colson that Baptist theologian Carl F. H. Henry cemented. Henry was Colson's fourth major influence. In 1977, Cromartie arranged a meeting for the two men. They soon became close. Colson loved studying history; Henry was living history. He used to begin his seminary classes at Trinity Evangelical Divinity School on the history of evangelical Christianity by giving his birthdate.[26]

This was not far from the truth. In the 1940s, with evangelist Billy Graham and pastor Harold Ockenga, Henry created what was called "neo-evangelicalism" to signal its movement away from fundamentalism. In short, the "neo-evangelicals" wanted to engage and dialogue with the culture, showing how the gospel answered a secular culture's questions. In the judgment of Henry and his peers, fundamentalists failed to engage the culture in a helpful manner, focusing their attention on such strenuous efforts at separation that they lost sight of being a gospel influence.

Henry was a towering figure in the evangelical world. When Colson met him in the mid-70s, he was in the midst of publishing his six-volume magnum opus, *God, Revelation, and Authority*. The book series made the case that the biblically revealed God was the intellectual and theological foundation the finite human person desperately needed. *GRA*, all three thousand densely argued pages of it, showed that Henry was a thinker with whom any self-respecting theologian had to deal.[27]

Henry was a scholar. He could more than handle his own in debates with European scholars like Karl Barth and Rudolph Bultmann. But he did not fit the stereotype of the isolated thinker. He was a journalist early in his career and never tired of the thrill of developing news. As a Christian, he was keenly interested in evangelism and discipleship. He taught Sunday school at Capitol Hill Metropolitan Baptist Church in Washington, DC, where he had moved to become the first editor of *Christianity Today* (1956–68).

Henry broke other stereotypes as well. He did not shy away from personal interaction, but regularly interrupted his speaking trips to witness to people he befriended. Years later, fellow church member Matt Schmucker remembered Henry's final trip to DC, a trip taken when Henry was frail but still insistent on making it to the Prison Fellowship board meeting.[28] Hours after Henry was supposed to arrive at the home of friends, the elderly theologian was found sharing the gospel with the pilot of the airplane that brought him to Washington. Henry was then in his late eighties. His elderly wife—back in Wisconsin—hadn't heard from him in hours and was frantic. But when Schmucker found Henry at a DC hotel, he saw immediately that Henry was glowing. Though a world-famous theologian, he was thrilled to have been able to share Christ with a fellow sinner.

Colson and Henry developed a close friendship, and Henry became the theological chair of Prison Fellowship for twenty years, serving on its board and giving theological instruction and reflection at meetings in Virginia. When Henry died in 2003, Colson gave testimony to his friend's formative role in his life:

In my earliest days as a Christian, Carl helped me develop my own theological understandings. After he joined Prison Fellowship's Board, he was the solid rock that kept us anchored to our faith. Carl was a former journalist, converted to Christ as a newsman (if there's hope for newsmen, there's hope for anybody!), and brought those great journalistic skills with him into the kingdom.[29]

Henry was a gracious mentor to Colson, the theologian's stern reputation notwithstanding: "I personally am forever in Carl's debt because he mentored me so lovingly. Not once in our close relationship over twenty years did he ever tell me anything; he was always very patient to explain that what I had said was very good, but then he asked if I had thought about another perspective." Colson, no intellectual slouch himself, concluded the point: "He was one of the great minds teaching a fledgling, and he did it with understanding, patience, love, humility."[30]

FRANCIS SCHAEFFER

The fifth major influence on Colson was Francis Schaeffer. Born in 1912 to a nominal Christian family in Virginia, Schaeffer was walking down the street of his hometown, feeling depressed and out of sorts, when he came upon a tent meeting led by an unknown evangelist. Just a few people were present, but as the gospel was preached, he was converted. Schaeffer later trained under confessional Presbyterian theologian J. Gresham Machen before moving for a time in a more fundamentalist direction through the influence of Carl McIntyre. Desiring to preach the cross to the spiritually starved children of Europe, Schaeffer moved to Switzerland with his gifted wife, Edith, in 1948. He never left.

In 1955, the Schaeffers founded L'Abri, a Christian teaching station and boarding home. *L'Abri* means "shelter" in French, and the unusual chalet-turned-chapel became, against all the odds, a world-famous spiritual waystation for people ranging from European travelers to disillusioned pastors' kids to rock stars like Eric Clapton to countercultural guru Timothy Leary.[31] Schaeffer had shifted theologically once more, believing that Christians needed to understand the culture and to empathize with lost people in order to evangelize effectively. His perspective was profoundly shaped by the sixteenth-century Reformers and by Abraham Kuyper.

Schaeffer seized upon this inspiring conviction. He found in it a divine commission to engage the arts and later the political realm. With his idiosyncratic dress and flowing beard, Schaeffer was a colorful figure in the buttoned-up world of conservative evangelicalism, but he won a wide hearing due to his persuasive presentation and his often-insightful cultural analysis. Like Colson, Schaeffer was a mesmerizing speaker. At one point, he went to Wheaton College and gave one of his classic lectures ranging over poetry, painting, and the fine arts. After charting the tragic state of the human condition without Christ, Schaeffer suddenly said, "There's death in the city; there's death in the city; there's death in the city." He then sat down, his audience buzzing from the staccato conclusion.[32] Schaeffer lectured in similar fashion at countless prestigious schools over his career, including Cambridge, Oxford, Harvard, and M.I.T.

Schaeffer's lectures left a mark on many, but he did not

confine his teaching to this format. His daylong conversation with Colson was one of many such conversations. Schaeffer would regularly talk all night with L'Abri visitors, answering their questions, putting on records for them to listen to, and praying lengthy petitions. Prayer was key; sometimes grace lasted for twenty minutes before the meals at L'Abri.

It was Schaeffer's model—blended with Wilberforce's—that Colson most emulated in his later career. He became a movement leader, an apologist, and a specialist in Christian worldview thinking. Colson never sought to be a theologian and did not describe himself in such terms. When Colson spent time around theologians like Sproul, Henry, Richard Lovelace, and others, he recognized that they had been given their own unique spheres of influence. But Colson did not react badly to his exposure to such friends. He neither cowered in their presence nor disdained them out of a sense of inferiority. Colson showed a remarkable willingness to learn and grow from his evangelical peers. Though he was much better known than any of them, he sat at their feet—or, in Schaeffer's case, ascended to their chalet.

Colson did not conduct his time of deeper research in a quiet place. He studied and learned while building a ministry from scratch that no one had foreseen. Colson changed greatly over the years, but even after his conversion, he remained the same hard-driving personality he had been. While working in a busy senator's office in the 1950s, Colson knocked out his law degree at George Washington. He did much the same in his post-conversion years, roaming the nation's prisons by day and conducting impromptu seminar and colloquia with top scholars on layovers. This was not the typical way of getting advanced training in history and theology, but one must remember: there was nothing typical about Chuck Colson.

All this reflection left a mark on Colson. For the rest of his days, he read and cited Kuyper, Wilberforce, Sproul, Henry, Schaeffer, and others, including C. S. Lewis and fellow ex-convicts Alexander Solzhenitsyn and Dietrich Bonhoeffer. This cadre of thinkers and leaders provided Colson with a circle of like-minded ministry partners with whom he could converse, whether in person or through their writings, and from whom he could gain inspiration when he grew weary or discouraged. Without his mentors, dead and living, Colson would still have been proficient in the activity of ministry, to be sure. He would have lacked, however, a council of advisors and a pantheon of heroes who had themselves taken up arduous and often lonely work for the glory of God.

Colson helped popularize these writers, in fact. His earliest books, *Born Again* (1976) and *Life Sentence* (1979), are both well written and rich in anecdotes and enlivening exhortations. But it was not until he entered his own makeshift seminary program that his thought matured and widened. His book *Loving God* (1983) reflects this intellectual progression. Written with Ellen Vaughan, it represents what many of Colson's books would provide in the next three decades: it is compelling, constructed around true stories told to dramatic effect, personal, and calibrated around life change. Colson and his cowriters excelled at boiling worldviews and philosophical arguments down to a nub, critiquing them, and showing how they affected day-to-day life. At the core, Colson wanted his readers to experience what he had tasted: the satisfaction of an existence devoted to God alone.

The Prison Fellowship founder had plunged into Christian ministry with his whole heart—just as he had worked in politics and law. Colson never did anything timidly or half-heartedly. *Loving God*, the fruit of a period of reflection on what mattered most, demonstrated Colson's desire for his fellow believers to break with a small vision of God and a small vision of the Christian life. Through Colson's study, he had discovered "a whole new vision of the majesty of the God we serve," which in turn created in him "a continuing desire for deeper knowledge."[33] He was not simply eager to do more ministry; he wanted to give a glorious God his entire being. He wanted not only to live obediently but also to think deeply about God, and to help many brothers and sisters do the same. He never became a full-time professor, but Colson lived a theologically driven life for the duration of his days.

Colson's trajectory is instructive for modern Christians. As he grew as a believer, he was not content to study the Bible at a basic level for the rest of his life. He placed himself at the feet of gifted teachers and leaders in an effort to learn from them. The goal of his education was not to out-argue people. It was not to heap up book learning to make conversation partners feel inferior. Colson recognized that in studying theology and history, he was learning more about God and the world he had made. This was the most valuable enterprise a person could undertake. What was more meaningful than beholding the glory of God as revealed in his Word?

As Christians, we should hunger for doctrinal "meat," not "milk," as the author of Hebrews made plain (5:12). A baby initially loves milk, but must graduate to a more complex diet. So it is for the church. Not only pastors but also the whole body of Christ should want to eat richer, more substantive spiritual food than we do when young in our faith. We might feel stuck and listless at times, though. If this is the case, Chuck Colson gives us a model of how to get going.

————

At the feet of several wise and godly tutors, Chuck Colson uncovered the exhilaration of a God-driven existence. He recognized, in a moment of humility, that the study of God and his world was not for the ivory tower. It was for the pew. Theology, he saw, is calibrated for action. Every Christian stands to benefit immeasurably from knowing God more. Making our way through a fallen world is not a quiet or calm experience, after all. We all need a foundation. We will be stronger believers, and more effective in ministry, when we have one.

Chuck Colson saw that he needed roots after becoming a Christian. In an array of faithful voices from the past and his present, he found them. He would draw on this theological foundation for the years to come. He would need it. He thought in his quieter moments that his life might soon calm down, and his ministry might adopt a more manageable pace.

In God's providence, it would soon expand beyond his wildest expectations.

FIVE

EXPANSION

Mary Kay Beard held the shotgun aloft. She was in her element. With her husband, Beard was robbing banks in one state after another. By 1972, her criminal exploits won her a place on the list of lists for notorious criminals: the FBI's Most Wanted.

Beard had not grown up aspiring to such infamy. The fifth of nine children, she was born in 1945 and raised on a farm in Alabama. Beard's mother was a devout Christian who did her best to train her kids in the ways of God. Her love, however, could not overcome Beard's anger. Her father was an alcoholic who took out his own anger on his family. By the time she was thirteen, her father had broken her nose twice. For weeks she experienced terrible pain after he punched her by surprise in the chest; later she found out he had broken her ribs.[1]

At age twenty-one, Beard was proficient with a gun and full of fury. She had learned to handle numerous firearms while growing up. After a failed marriage that produced two children, Beard married a man she met on a blind date. Her initial happiness was soon overcome by surprise: six months after their wedding, she discovered her new spouse was skilled in the dark art of robbery. He trained Beard to crack safes and rob banks.[2] She loved breaking into safes, though she was equally good at wielding a double-barreled sawed-off shotgun. She later called it her "specialty."[3]

In June 1972, just months before Chuck Colson entered prison, Beard was arrested. Federal authorities brought eleven federal indictments and thirty-five charges against her. She was sentenced to twenty-one years in prison.[4] Beard went to the Julia Tutwiler Prison for Women in Birmingham a lost soul, angry and despairing.

She began to attend a Sunday morning Bible class held at seven o'clock. At one of the meetings she asked a prison ministry volunteer, "Why do you bother?" It was a hostile question but a genuine one. The woman responded, "Jesus loved you enough to go all the way to Calvary; we love you enough to come and tell you about him."[5] Beard was taken aback. She remained silent but kept attending the classes. Her interest in spiritual things was growing. She began reading a Bible left by the Gideons in the prison. Externally, she kept up a tough front; internally, she was churning.

Beard found to her surprise that she could not turn away from the Bible. Years after her prison sentence, she read Ezekiel 36:26–27: "I will give you a new heart and put a new spirit within you; I will remove the heart of stone from your flesh and give you a heart of flesh. And I will put my Spirit within you and cause you to walk in My statutes, and you will be careful to observe My ordinances."[6] In that moment, reading the Gideon Bible, Mary Kay came to the end of herself. "In a flash of revelation," she

later noted, "I recognized the Truth of those words." She prayed
to God to save her.

Beard may have been in jail, but she was born again. In days
to come, her story would take another twist. Though neither one
then knew the other, ex-cons Mary Kay Beard and Chuck Colson
would soon team up to minister grace to prisoners' families on
an unprecedented scale.

———

Prison can be a deadening time. Against the odds, Beard came
alive during it. At Christmas one year, Beard noticed unusual interest in religious services among her fellow inmates.
Christian groups came to the jail and conducted services for the
prisoners. Inmates "who never went to a chapel program always
went to those programs" for one reason, according to Beard:
they wanted to get the free gifts given out by the evangelicals.[7]
Beard was skeptical about the program. The prisoners seemed to
be interested only in material things. But as Beard watched her
fellow prisoners, she discovered the true reason for their interest
in the little gifts:

> Initially I was rather cynical about that, but then I noticed
> that the women would take those gifts and they would give
> them to their own children. The gifts were just little bits of
> toiletry items: a bar of soap, a tube of toothpaste. And they
> would take those and wrap them up for their kids.
>
> I realized that a mother's heart doesn't really change
> toward her children, even when she has broken the law in

many other ways. It's still the heart of a mother to give to her children and sacrifice her own needs.[8]

Beard had made a priceless discovery. The prisoners were not hoarding the little toothpaste tubes and small bars of soap, as she had first thought. They took the toiletries, wrapped them up, and either sent them to their children or, even better, gave the tiny presents to their kids during visitation times. At first, Mary Kay feared that she was witnessing an act of selfishness. In reality, she was witnessing the ongoing presence of selflessness in her fellow inmates.

When the children of these women received their gifts, Mary Kay was again surprised. She thought the little boys and girls who visited their mothers in prison would take the opportunity to express annoyance over their tiny, little Christmas gift; other kids, after all, were given Barbies and Legos. The opposite was true. Getting a bar of soap meant the world to these children. Their faces lit up when they visited their mothers, and they were grateful for their small presents. Rarely had toothpaste—the bane of many a wriggling toddler—been more appreciated by a child.

Something had switched on in Mary Kay. Once angry and violent, she was a transformed woman. She had been a quick study in crime; now she proved a prodigy in the discipline of education. Six years in to her sentence, Beard was paroled. In short order, she earned a bachelor's degree in secondary education and a master's in counseling. Mary Kay was on the right track, but she did not know how she would serve the Lord.

It was at this point that the paths of Colson and Beard intertwined. Colson had heard Mary Kay's story through his network of prison-ministry associates. The Prison Fellowship maestro offered Beard the role of Alabama state director in 1982.[9] She was tasked with coordinating a Christmas project for inmates but hesitated at first to physically reenter Alabama jails. As she later joked, she "had already been there" and did not wish at that early juncture to go back. Beard decided to do something different: she decided to start a program to send gifts to the children of prisoners. Crest and Colgate were great, but Beard thought she could do better.

It took a nasty comment to put Beard's benevolent insight in motion. In her role, Mary Kay spoke to many groups across Alabama, seeking to spread awareness and raise support for the ministry. At one such event in 1982, one woman expressed the view that prisoners should be locked up and the key thrown away. This perspective crossed classes, political affiliations, and religions in America; it may well be the leading philosophy on prison in this country. Like Colson, Beard bristled at this suggestion. If the key had been thrown away, and rehabilitation impossible, she would have been wearing a prison uniform, not a dress with pearls. Her kids would have been left without a mother. Beard responded to the woman by sharing how devastating conviction was for the children of inmates. This softened her audience, and in particular, the woman who had expressed herself strongly.

The two struck up a conversation after Beard's presentation. Beard came away with the idea to run a small campaign at a local mall to bless the children of inmates with Christmas gifts. She decided to put up a Christmas tree in both Birmingham and Montgomery to prompt shoppers to buy presents for the children in question. A friend had the idea to go just a little further:

to write the names of children on little angel-shaped paper ornaments. Shoppers would claim an "angel" to support.

Mary Kay contacted prisoners she knew to close the loop,
telling them, "If you will give me the names and addresses of
where your children are, I will do my best to get them Christmas."
She wanted to reach several hundred kids but had little sense of
what would transpire. The Christmas trees went up, the ornaments—red for girls, green for boys—were created, and "Angel
Tree" was launched.[10]

The program was brilliantly conceived. The name quickly
caught on, the ornaments were a whimsical yet personal touch,
and the public responded in force when Angel Tree debuted in
Birmingham on "Black Friday." In a matter of hours, Birmingham
shoppers purchased all one hundred of the ornaments. Shocked,
Beard went into action, calling more prisons, setting up more
requests for gifts, and carefully cutting out more little angels,
each of them representing a child who would undoubtedly know
a happier Christmas than he or she otherwise might have. In
1982, 556 children received gifts. Angel Tree was an immediate
success.[11]

The program grew quietly over the years. In its second
year, it expanded into twelve states. The early Angel Tree was
a work in progress. It had not begun in an extended strategy
session with the Colson brain trust. It was not the result of a
carefully crafted effort to win good PR for Prison Fellowship.
Angel Tree began because an ex-convict wanted to minister
to the families of prisoners. Despite these humble, almost
accidental, beginnings, it became a mighty engine for mercy
ministry. Beard later described the gentle momentum of Angel
Tree's ministry:

Many times, inmates rather tentatively give that name to the volunteers, not really believing that their child will receive Christmas gifts. Then, in January and February, our Bible studies in prison doubled and tripled in size because inmates would come to the door of the chapel and say, "Is this the bunch that bought Christmas for my child?"[12]

This pattern repeated itself thousands and thousands of times over the years. Angel Tree was not coercive. It worked with a demographic well aware of false promises and broken trust. Prisoners would not buy in to a program that used them, manipulated them, or sold them false hope. They were an inherently skeptical crowd. But Angel Tree's formula was brilliant, owing not to an organizational strategy but to the inquisitive mind of an ex-con.

Beard understood the psychology of inmates. She knew that women (and later many men) would initially struggle to trust the system. Buying in to the Angel Tree model meant that inmates had to give out private information—the names of their children. This was a momentous step, but a meaningful one. If inmates trusted the volunteers with the names of their children, they had taken an initial step toward trusting the ministry more generally. No doubt the vast majority of prisoners waited to see if the Christian group would back up its claims. The world knows no shortage of religious types who promise one thing and deliver another. But Angel Tree, driven by Mary Kay Beard and a growing number of compassionate volunteers, made good on its word. As a result, many inmates who had expressed hostility toward Christianity eventually attended Bible studies.

Perhaps the most interesting part of the project was that the ministry volunteers did not meet the inmates. They obtained the information they needed through the chaplaincy network. When the ministry showed that it would follow through on its commitments, inmates responded. Beard made this clear: "They came, really, out of a sense of obligation. But they stayed and heard the Gospel. Indirectly, we realized that it's an awesome tool of evangelism to the inmates. The inmates never see the volunteers, yet by reaching out to the children, God also reaches back to their parent."[13] Many prisoners first engaged with Angel Tree to better connect with their children. In the process, many connected with the living God.

Angel Tree was a runaway success wherever it was implemented in the first five years of its existence. Yet it stayed small during this time. Mary Kay Beard did not promote her own work, and others did not seize on the immense potential of the operation until 1986, when it came across Colson's radar. The story of this connection speaks to how Colson was able to use his celebrity for good ends. Colson came out to Montgomery, Alabama, to "promote and observe" Angel Tree in its early days. He was scheduled to interview a little boy on television about the program. The boy's mother was in prison, and this prompted the following exchange:

> Chuck talked with the oldest boy, helping him become comfortable with the microphone and lights. He told the boy how Christmas is about Jesus.
>
> "Jesus is God's Son and He came to save all of us from our sins. If we ask Jesus to come into our hearts, we can live with Him in heaven forever. Have you ever done that?"
>
> "No," said the little boy.

"Well, would you like to do that?" Chuck didn't really expect any response.

"Now?"

"If you want."

The boy reached over and put his little hand in Chuck's big one and said, "Uh, huh."

Chuck, choked with emotion, prayed with the boy. When it was time to film, Chuck asked him, "What is the most important Christmas gift?" The boy was supposed to respond, "Jesus."

But he said, "To have my Mommy home for Christmas." A tear rolled down the boy's face, and his three-year-old sister reached up, patted her brother on the cheek, and wiped the tear. Everyone watching in the mall, including Chuck, began weeping.[14]

At this point, Colson embraced Angel Tree wholeheartedly. He soon urged the Prison Fellowship board to make Angel Tree a national program and later an international one. The board did, and ninety thousand gifts were given out that season.[15] The momentum did not stop there. During the next several years, Colson continued to advocate for Beard's initiative. By the early 1990s, Angel Tree giving was almost literally through the roof of the Prison Fellowship headquarters in Reston, Virginia, as presents filled every corner and desk. Today, more than thirty years after the program had begun, Angel Tree estimates that the ministry has served more than nine million children.[16]

Colson did not found Angel Tree. He always stated that up front when asked about the ministry, giving generous credit to Mary Kay Beard. He did, however, act as an accelerant. Colson saw the tremendous promise of the program and moved to make good on it. By the mid-1980s, when Colson first noticed the great success of the early phase of Angel Tree, he had the organizational heft to catapult it ahead. When he used his cache to do so, the results were immediate and dramatic.

During successive decades, Angel Tree drew continual praise, sometimes from surprising voices. In 2012, Colson did a *BreakPoint* radio segment in which he told the story of a prisoner named Rick. Rick had connected with Angel Tree years earlier to send his daughter Christmas presents during his five-year sentence. When Rick's daughter came to visit him after Christmas, she was thrilled. She wasn't alone. The children of a number of inmates who belonged to the Nation of Islam visited them following Christmas. Rick found to his surprise that the children of Muslims were, like his daughter, raving about their gifts. It seems that these men—none of whom celebrated Christmas—had taken the unique opportunity provided by Angel Tree to send their own progeny a package. In some cases, the children reported, the gifts came from "white churches."

Colson reflected on the reaction of the prisoners: "They could scarcely believe that not only had Christian churches been willing to help children of another faith, they were also demonstrating love for children of another race."[17] Angel Tree had not only brightened a dreary holiday for some lonely kids. It led numerous men, Rick reported, to investigate the claims of Christianity. Here were Christians who were standing in the gap, helping Muslim men—men whose theology they did not share—connect with their loved ones. The ability of this unique program to break through barriers regularly surprised even those who led it.

Beard's program found a way to reconnect broken people. It repaired familial fabric that was devastated by crime. The cycle of brokenness begins with sin. From there, dysfunction easily spreads. Without a stable home situation, characterized by a dependable father and mother, children come to dislike the very institutions created by God to unleash human flourishing and curate human dignity. The home, ordained for stability and nurture, becomes a symbol of pain. The police, ordained to protect and help, become adversaries. The church, ordained to preach and bind up, seems shallow and ineffectual. The government, ordained to respect and strengthen the populace, seems corrupt and self-enriching. When the home suffers, the reputation and regard of other God-given institutions suffer as well.

There is a lesson here for the church today. Thirty years after the founding of Angel Tree, the church has the chance to strengthen the family. This is what Beard did: she saw how prisoners were isolated from their children, and she worked to reconnect them. We can do the same. To do so, we will have to reach out to people. We cannot strengthen and rebuild broken homes by keeping to ourselves. Whether entering jails, coaching sports, or mentoring kids after school, we can minister grace to families torn apart by suffering and sin.

Nowadays, many younger Christians want to change the world. Too few of us, however, are active in our local communities. We find ourselves in an odd predicament: we want to revolutionize society, but we can't find the time or energy to get involved in our own neighborhoods. I'm reminded of the saying that popped up in the revolutionary heyday of years past: "Everybody wants to save the world, but nobody wants to do the dishes." In seeking to love our neighbor and repair hurting families, we often do not need to reconceive ministry. Instead, we should consider plugging into the institutions God has created for our benefit: family, church, school, community, and civic life. We should do the small things. We should, you could say, wash the dishes.

We should also recognize the transformative power of the family itself. One of the best settings for activism is our own family. As spouses, as parents, we should recognize that we *are* activists, whether we know this or not. Many times we fail to see just how important our own familial health is. I found an example of this truth in a recent story of a young father in Camden, New Jersey, who started a baseball league for neighborhood boys, most of whom had never met their fathers.[18] As they joined his team, they gained a vision of what a father should be. This young man became a father figure to children who had no other image of a dad. Even just one stable, happy family on a street can be transformative for the neighborhood.

The church needs to operate from this kind of perspective. Healthy marriages and happy children are evangelistic. As millennial Christians, all around us are young people who think that happiness comes through hedonism. Young married couples who are raising children are a powerful rebuke to this view. We are not only offering arguments, we're displaying them—in the form of little children whom we regard as blessings, not a curse. Against the culture of death, we celebrate life, tangible life in the form of little boys and girls who obey and love their parents. Our activism is day-by-day, step-by-step, meal-by-meal. It is small. It is sometimes ordinary, even rote. But it matters.

Young Christians are rarely more revolutionary than when we cultivate strong marriages according to the biblical design.

Men are called to fill the roles of self-sacrificial, Christlike "heads," and women joyfully submit to men as a picture of the church's love for Jesus (Eph. 5:22–33).[19] Fathers can not only sire children but order their lives around courageous, self-sacrificial leadership of their families. The health of our families is the cornerstone of our social activism, after all. If evangelical families are weak, then we should expect that our reform efforts will be weak. God *should not* bless Christians who give little attention to their loved ones. If our marriages flag and our kids despise us, we cannot fault our non-Christian neighbors for tuning us out.

When the family is thriving, it is a force for good. There is nothing in natural terms that produces better personal health and social good than this. As a young father now, I seek to lovingly instruct and guide my three children. I know that I am increasingly an anomaly. Many of my peers have not yet settled down. Though in their thirties, they're still chasing happiness in something other than what most were created for: the family. They have not yet come to see that, while we will never experience ultimate satisfaction in family life, God has intended that we derive tremendous happiness from it. The stability and sturdiness of the natural family is a precious gift. By reaching out to those around us in need, and by cultivating our own bonds, we can extend the legacy of past Christians and work to repair the fabric of the family in our time.

This is true of every believer, young or old. Whether we are single or married, we can minister the gospel, exhibit the power of the Christian family, and repair homes wrecked by sin. Led by Beard and championed by Colson, Angel Tree worked in just these kinds of ways. It strengthened institutions. It reconnected and repaired families. It began to restore trust where it had died out. Angel Tree brought cynical prisoners into contact with their families but also with the local church and its transformative gospel. In helping to reform individuals through its simple program, Angel Tree rehabilitated the prisoners' view of the home and the church.

Not every story related to Angel Tree was so dramatic, of course. In the 1980s, Colson's broader ministry was indeed ramping up. By 1986, Prison Fellowship had drawn hundreds of donors and had a budget of more than $12 million by 1986. The organization employed more than two hundred staff, including twenty-one state or regional directors, and marshaled a veritable army of volunteers to support its efforts.[20] In 1976, after Colson told Patty that they would go into "every prison in the country," they might have wondered if they overshot the moon. By the late 1980s, this statement seemed inadequate. The Colsons as a ministry pair were bent on entering every prison *in the world*.

The on-the-ground work of Prison Fellowship continued apace, staging more than four hundred in-prison seminars in America per year. At the same time, Prison Fellowship International went full-steam ahead. Founded in 1979, PFI's existence signaled that the ministry was indeed a global one, with thriving chapters in countries like England, Scotland, France, and New Zealand.

With Prison Fellowship, PFI, Angel Tree, Justice Fellowship, and several other smaller initiatives to manage, the ministry Colson founded and led had grown beyond belief. It functioned on several levels: training prison staffers, engaging prisoners directly, touching the lives of prisoners' families, advocating for prison reform, and involving an ever-increasing number of pastors and local churches in prison ministry.

Colson managed this colossus of activity not from a quiet

office but from the tarmac, the taxicab, and the talk-and-walk meeting. He was known for dictating one memo after another, frequently while boarding a plane, and not infrequently over the objections of stewardesses who thought it preferable to offer executive leadership while on the ground. All the while, Colson wrote, spoke, held meetings, and did media appearances. Though he did not love asking people for money, he excelled at the task, bringing in over ten million dollars a year by the mid-1980s. Yet the budget was still a fraction of what its height—around $50 million—would reach in the twenty-first century.

This heavy workload took a toll on Colson. Even as he poured himself into the work of prison ministry, in 1987 he experienced the health scare of his life. He was in Manila to speak at several places in the Philippines when he was seized with wrenching cramps. Hemorrhaging blood, he was diagnosed with a bleeding ulcer, which initially led the ever-sanguine, ever-peripatetic Colson to reason that he could move on with his densely packed speaking schedule. The initial diagnosis was in a way correct: he did have an ulcer. He also, however, had a cancerous tumor that "had punched a hole in my stomach wall," as he later reflected.[21] In a flash, Colson's life came to a thudding halt. Though his family did not fully know it, Colson was in a fight for his survival.

In January 1987, Colson went into surgery. He expected to be out of the hospital in less than a week. Instead, following a painful and intensive operation, he contracted a staph infection, the scourge of hospitals. For the next four weeks, Colson was in and out of consciousness, fighting ferocious pain and nighttime delusions. At one point he looked at Emily and shouted, "Emily, you're growing whiskers!"[22] As the fifty-five-year-old surfed the pain surging through his body, he found himself thinking about his family.

Colson's early-1970s period of conversion and Christian growth meant improvement in his relationship with his three children: Wendell, Christian, and Emily. His kids loved him, and he loved them. He had communicated this with greater attentiveness since coming to Christ. It was not until Colson's terrible illness that he and Emily talked extensively and honestly about spiritual matters. Colson later remembered the period as an impactful one: "I prayed with her frequently, and I could often see tears in her eyes as I did."[23] Both father and daughter relished this quiet, if difficult, season.

Cancer was a formidable foe. Though Colson's life hung in the balance throughout the winter of 1987, he pulled through. Emily and her father gained through cancer what normal life had never allowed: a great deal of time together spent navigating a terrific challenge. Emily nursed her father gradually back to health, talking with him, praying with him, wiping his face down with a cool cloth when he grew feverish. After Colson left the hospital, he soon found the tables turned. Emily's husband left her and their eighteen-month-old autistic son, Max. The pain of this desertion tore into Emily, leaving her raw and vulnerable. Now it was Chuck's turn to care for Emily. He would not abandon his daughter.

Redemption was active not only in Colson's life but in the lives of others touched by Prison Fellowship. One of the most dramatic turnarounds Colson witnessed was in the life of a man named Danny Croce. Croce was the kind of guy Colson instinctively gravitated toward. He was from Brockton, Massachusetts, a working-class town that produced scrappy figures like boxer "Marvelous" Marvin Hagler, Al Davis of the "win baby win" Oakland Raiders, and Shawn Fanning of Napster. Croce himself emulated Hagler and fought professionally. He was short, but tough as raw leather.

Croce was drawn not only to the exhilaration of professional fighting but to the momentary peaks provided by drugs. He was, like so many young men, chasing experiences, eager to prove himself. He later remembered his sorry state: "I had smoked for almost 20 years. Then we went to marijuana, free-basing cocaine, drinking, gambling and swearing."[24] On the night that undid Croce, he had been freebasing cocaine with his friend Sully. The two were ironworkers. They prided themselves on their physical work and their ability to handle hard substances. Danny was known for drinking a six-pack at lunch and then climbing into the sky to hang girders on Boston skyscrapers.

The alcohol was a constant. In February 1984, Croce and his buddies went barhopping. Danny was the driver. On his way home, Danny lost control of his car, drove through a wooden barrier, and smashed into a policeman named John Gilbert, carrying him thirty yards down the road. Gilbert died instantly from his injuries. Danny had killed a friend, a man who had watched him box, and who served his community.[25] He was devastated.

When Danny was sentenced, he did not plead innocent. He pled guilty to the charges, much like Colson. In February 1985, he entered the Plymouth County Correctional Facility in Plymouth, Massachusetts. He was full of guilt and shame. As with many prisoners, he struggled to sleep. He joined a vehicular-homicide group in the prison. It was supposed to provide support, but it left him dry. When Danny shared his story, his peers said of Gilbert, "It was his time. Everyone's ticket gets punched." The words did nothing to help Danny. He was tormented by guilt.

A man came up to Danny after the meeting, however, and asked him a simple question: "Have you ever prayed to God?" Danny had not prayed since childhood. He began praying, and he started studying the Bible with the man. As he read the Gospels, he felt himself simultaneously horrified by God's judgment of sin and entranced by Jesus. He attended chapel, and through the message and his Bible reading, Danny saw that he was a sinner, vile and unclean, but even more importantly that Jesus was the Savior, righteous and forgiving. Not long after he went to chapel, he knelt by himself in his jail cell and prayed to Jesus to save him. That night, for the first time in a long time, he slept well.[26]

Danny's world intersected with Colson's when Christmas came around. He had nothing for his little girl. A staffer from Angel Tree came to Plymouth and told the inmates about their program. Danny couldn't believe that the organization would send out brand-new gifts. This was unheard of. Angel Tree followed through on its promise, and Melissa Croce had a happy Christmas. Not long after, in 1986, Danny was released from prison. He had committed his life to the Lord, and he dedicated himself to his family, his job, and earning his college degree. He was able to fulfill the last because of a scholarship to Wheaton College established by Charles W. Colson.

Danny's life was restored. He had a hunger to know his Savior. But as the years passed, something was missing. He had an itch. He needed to get back to Plymouth. He eventually did, becoming a chaplain at his former prison in 1996. Danny worked alongside the men who had led him to Christ, and he himself was able to lead other men to Christ. One inmate gave such evidence of conversion that a prison guard stopped him and asked him to tell him about Jesus. In 2002, Danny became the head chaplain at Plymouth, ministering to more than fourteen hundred inmates.[27] The work was not and is not easy, but Danny Croce—like Chuck Colson—was not looking for easy work. He was looking to serve the lost and desperate on behalf of Christ's kingdom.[28]

The grace of God rested on Danny's work. It also rested on Colson's work. His unflagging zeal for prison ministry led him in a few years' time to become America's leading evangelical figure in this sector. His work was unusually successful. Colson could add new projects to his increasingly well-funded outfit, amplify the work of an outstanding program like Angel Tree, and personally fund the studies of an ex-convict whom God had profoundly converted. This was unusual influence powered by uncommon grace.

Evangelical statesman Gregory Thornbury, president of the King's College, later said of Colson's work in prisons that "Prison Fellowship was the way that he showed the world that the gospel was real."[29] Thornbury's summation rings true. Every time Colson entered a prison, he was acting on the conviction that Christ loved and would save sinners. For this reason, Colson loved prison work. No fair-minded observer could charge him with engaging in evangelism for a profit. He went to prisons and labored in innumerable ways to aid prisoners because he relished the opportunity. Whether or not his fellow evangelicals would join him, Colson would go. He went because God would meet him there. God always had work for him to do.

Colson knew the power of conversion. He understood that

many prisoners considered themselves hopeless, and that many people in the broader society shared that opinion of them. But he did not. He had tasted amazing grace, as the former slave trader John Newton called it, and he wanted others to taste it too. To make this happen, however, someone had to constantly look for opportunities. Ministering to inmates was a major challenge. In a program like Angel Tree, Colson found a spiritual foothold that could propel gospel work in prisons across the world.

We do not all have Chuck Colson's vision and leadership abilities. We may not all be able to green-light a new gospel outreach overnight or chair a board meeting that changes the face of evangelistic work. But we all have a conscience. The Holy Spirit has given us all a love for others. It does not take organizational genius to start ministering to needy people in our communities. One need not be a CEO to love one's neighbor in tangible ways. Mary Kay Beard simply had her eyes open. She wondered why her fellow inmates were so interested in Christmas services in her jail. When she discovered they attended them to receive gifts to give their children, she found a gospel opportunity. The same can be true for us as we open our eyes to the needs around us.

It is encouraging to consider how often God uses unexpected people to glorify his name. No one was predicting when Mary Kay was a prisoner that she would jump-start a program that would come to the attention of a US president. Decades before George W. Bush made Angel Tree programs a key part of his regular Christmas visits to needy children, Mary Kay was a convict. She wasn't educated. She wasn't being fast-tracked for leadership. She hadn't even finished her jail sentence. She was, however, born again. That made her, in just the right sense, a dangerous person indeed. The providence of God never misses its target. It was precisely because Mary Kay was a convict that she was able to spot a need among her fellow prisoners.

So it was for Danny Croce. He heard the gospel when he was at his lowest point. He was redeemed at a time when the kindest encouragement did nothing to salve his guilt. He knew that he had done terrible things, and he knew he deserved to feel shame over them. Self-help and positive thinking cannot take away such pain and despair. What Danny needed, only the gospel could give. Once he was born again, Danny was able to return to the prison that had contained him and help men whose hope, like his, was long since exhausted.

The church does not need savants. It needs faithful witnesses willing to do hard work to minister grace to needy sinners. As we labor, we remember that there are no limits to what God can do in our midst. Heaven submits to no design specifications. Grace operates according to no preconditions. The Lord can take a fallen White House staffer, a bank robber, and a drunk driver and make them agents of otherworldly salvation. There is no fast track to such influence. We can prepare for ministry, and we should whenever possible. But God never more shows his mysterious wisdom than in the men and women he appoints to service in his kingdom.

Sometimes, our efforts fall short. We have no guarantee of success. But in many cases, the Lord is pleased to amplify our humble offerings. He takes our small investment and expands it many times over. This was Chuck Colson's experience over the course of his Christian life. Success did not mean a fat paycheck and an easy life. It meant hard work, ministry expansion, and leadership on contested public-square issues.

It meant, in sum, being a witness.

SIX

WITNESS

Chuck Colson was hiding. An executive from Saab US, the carmaker, was on the line, but Colson told his assistant, "You take the call."[1] In Chuck Colson's dramatic, wide-ranging life, this episode stands out.

The occasion for this unexpected call was a Colson radio commentary. His *BreakPoint* program had been going strong for years and had several million listeners. Colson and the staff who helped compile and edit his commentaries had known for some time that many Christians listened to the four-minute program. But to this point, Colson's radio musings had not seriously affected the advertising campaign of an international automobile company.

The context for this strange development was Saab's 1995 "Find Your Own Road" marketing message. The press release from the company made an appeal to unconventional and independent car buyers: "By celebrating the spirit of individuality, Saab's Find Your Own Road campaign has struck a familiar chord in both longtime and first-time Saab enthusiasts." The only unifying thread among Saab buyers was their "strong passion for products that take a slightly different path from the mainstream."[2]

The "Find Your Own Road" ads were popular with the unified nonconformists who bought Saabs. The series was voted the most popular of any that the carmaker ever produced.[3] When Colson chanced across the commercials, however, he was not so inspired. He voiced his concerns to his *BreakPoint* listeners on July 30, 1997: "The Saab ads tap into a dream of baby boomers since the 1960s: the dream of 'doing your own thing.' During the sixties, the young idealists of the counterculture viewed authority as an impediment to personal authenticity." This generation wanted to be their own guide, according to Colson.[4]

After Colson's initial broadcast criticizing Saab's "existential philosophy of the sixties," the American president of Saab, Joel Manby, called Colson.

"Mr. Colson, I heard your radio program," Manby said.

"Yes, I suspected you might," Colson replied.

"I want to tell you. We have been reviewing our ad campaign, and you made a very good point. I had never thought about it. We were selling a philosophy, not cars. You won't see those 'find your own road' ads anymore."

Colson noted two years later in his 1999 commencement address at Gordon-Conwell Theological Seminary that he "never did" see the Saab ads again.[5] For the *BreakPoint* host, the takeaway was clear: "With God's help, we must embolden ourselves" and "challenge these falsehoods ourselves," wherever believers might find them. Alongside Ivy League professors, Hollywood directors, and governing officials, Swedish advertisers were served their notice: Chuck Colson would back down from no man.

For fifteen years, Colson had worked in prison ministry. In 1991, he launched a new phase of his work, beginning the Wilberforce Forum (later the Chuck Colson Center for Christian Worldview) in Reston, Virginia. The Center, located less than an hour from Washington, DC, became the clearinghouse for numerous initiatives within Prison Fellowship, the umbrella organization. One of the longest lasting and most impactful is the radio program *BreakPoint*. This was the second broadcast Colson attempted; *Another Point of View* had briefly aired years earlier. *BreakPoint* was not a long show, clocking in at around four minutes apiece, but it hugely amplified Colson's voice. The innovative format and quick-hitting topics showed that Colson was not only a good speaker but an intellectual entrepreneur capable of speaking to most any audience.

BreakPoint was tailor-made for Colson. It allowed him to pounce on an issue, succinctly dissect it, and respond to it with a bold call to evangelical action. Colson's distinctive voice went out all over America, eventually reaching more than fourteen hundred radio outlets. He did not so much talk as sling words from his mouth, and though his Boston patois softened over the years, he never lost his distinctive accent. The program offered its listeners a remarkable synthesis of material, ranging over philosophy, science, entertainment, and theology. Colson and his writing team considered these matters from a worldview perspective.

Colson had begun serious, self-directed studies of theology, history, and philosophy in the late 1970s. His broad reading and tutelage from figures like Carl Henry, R. C. Sproul, and Francis Schaeffer moved his own speaking and writing in the direction of worldview engagement. Colson did not wish to be a theologian, historian, philosopher, or cultural critic in the strict academic sense of these words. Instead, he blended these disciplines, zeroing in on two major themes: how Christianity as a system of thought and action brought salvation and flourishing, and how all non-Christian worldviews—beliefs that shaped all of life—ultimately failed at the spiritual, intellectual, and societal levels. Only God and his wisdom could re-enchant fallen humanity and restore corrupted cultures.

These fundamental convictions animated Colson's cultural engagement. He was called to be a witness. He believed that the West had reached a crisis point by the late 1980s and early 1990s. A once-great culture was eroding, and people were suffering as a result. This was what the Greeks would call a *kairos* moment—an hour of choosing, a time when the situation in America and the West had grown dire. It was left to persons of courage to speak and to act. In several books, *BreakPoint*, and the organization of Evangelical and Catholics Together, we witness Colson's efforts to broaden his own program beyond prison ministry and to take his place in the great public-square debate over the future of American hearts and minds.

Colson was not a culture warrior. He does not fit neatly into the hard-and-fast categories of late-twentieth-century American politics. His positions on a number of issues might seem to qualify Colson for membership in the Religious Right, and no small number of articles and watchdog groups would see him as such. Colson was a friend to many members of the Religious Right, to be sure; Hugh Hewitt, host of the *Hugh Hewitt Show*, said that "he was in it but not of it," an apt characterization.[6] Colson was not primarily or preeminently interested in "taking America back," per stereotypes of some evangelicals. He made this plain to the many hundreds of thousands of people looking to him for guidance.

One young evangelical was deeply impressed by Colson's carefully crafted political views. Andrew Walker, director of policy studies for the Ethics and Religious Liberty Commission of the Southern Baptist Convention, recalled meeting Colson and asking him to sign his copy of *God and Government* (2007). Colson gladly signed it: "To Andrew: Love your country, but love your God more. Chuck." Walker, since profiled by the *New York Times* and other outlets as a young Christian leader, noted that this represents an ideal way to summarize Christian public-square work. "It isn't an overstatement to say that I, and other Christians like me, motivated by a deep love of the gospel and a concern for culture, are trying to retrieve the Colsonian legacy for a new day—a day that's as badly in need of the gospel as Chuck once was."[7]

Walker's words nicely summarize Colson's basic commitments. He was keenly concerned about his country, but his mission was spiritual more than national. It was not the electoral college of America that most occupied Chuck Colson, but its soul. He saw how corrupt ideology and bad ideas stood to lead men and women away from the truth, from God, and how this non-Christian thinking would filter into all facets of society and culture if unchecked. Though he had common concerns with some members of the Religious Right, his major interest was in ideas, not politics.

The starting point for a discussion of Colson's worldview engagement should begin with the first major political text of the thirty total books he would publish. In *Kingdoms in Conflict* (1987), he sought with cowriter Ellen Santilli Vaughn to call the church to engage with the public square. He made the point straightforwardly, calling the church to be a force for good: "The influence of the Kingdom of God in the public arena is good for society as a whole."[8] Colson had a balanced view of this work. He noted that "the church was ordained principally for the conversion of men and women—conversion grounded in individual conscience wrought by the supernatural work of a sovereign God upon the soul." Yet he cautioned those who would read this primary mission as the privatization of Christianity: the church "is not to ignore the political scene." Instead, "through the individual Christian's involvement in politics . . . the standards of civic righteousness can be influenced by the standards of righteousness of the Kingdom of God."[9]

Colson's reading of thinkers like Augustine, Aquinas, and Martin Luther chastened his expansive vision of Christian influence on society. He noted that "tension between church and state is inherent and inevitable. Indeed, it is . . . part of the dynamic by which He governs His universe." Both institutions were needed for human flourishing, Colson argued. "To maintain this balance the church and the state must fulfill their respective roles. One cannot survive without the other; yet neither can do the work of the other. Both operate under God's rule, each in a different relationship to that rule."[10] Colson wanted the church to be the church: a force for spiritual *and* social good.

The solution would come from the church understanding afresh what it was and what it was to do. "The church," Colson argued, "is no civic center, no social club or encounter group, no Sunday morning meeting place. It is a new society, created for the salvation of a lost world, pointing to the kingdom to come."[11] This society stretched over all the world as the universal church, but was found in particular places, or local churches. Joining a local church was for Colson "the first step of discipleship," for it was in such a setting "where the Word is taught and sacraments administered."[12]

Colson himself was a faithful member of his own local church. When he lived in the DC area, he was a member of Columbia Baptist Church in Falls Church, Virginia. When he moved south, he was a longtime member of the First Baptist Church of Naples, Florida. Hayes Wicker, Colson's pastor in Naples, later reflected on Colson as a church member: "When Chuck joined our church, I urged him to teach a class for non-members, titled 'Why Believe?' It became the basis of his book *How Now Shall We Live?* and gave credibility to our new ministry."[13]

Wicker noted that Colson took notes during his sermons and would be in church on Sunday morning "even if he came in on a plane at midnight" the night before.[14] Colson's fellow church member John Michael LaRue confirmed this pattern. "He would sit in the same pew, right in front of me, and you would never have known that he was a major leader," LaRue said. "He would shake your hand, talk with you, and ask you how you were. He was kind and involved."[15] After the service, Colson regularly called Wicker to encourage him: "He had an extraordinary ability to encourage people," Wicker later said. "I never had a church member that so lifted me up and encouraged me."[16]

EVANGELICALS AND CATHOLICS TOGETHER

Colson loved the church. It was his desire that it be unified in order to promote good and oppose evil. In 1994, this instinct produced a project called Evangelicals and Catholics Together

(ECT). ECT brought together Protestant and Catholic theologians for the ultimate purpose of finding theological and sociopolitical unity where it could be had. ECT drew fire over the years, not least for its 1997 statement on the doctrine of justification, "The Gift of Salvation" (TGS). Some of Colson's fellow Protestants argued that it compromised a Reformation-informed understanding of the justification of the believer. TGS proved to be the most controversial of ECT's statements, all of which demand fuller treatment.

ECT was not a perfect project. It did, however, launch a bold and far-reaching program to strengthen the collective witness of the Christian tradition in America. It was forged out of friendship as much as theology. Colson had forged a strong bond with Richard John Neuhaus, a leading Catholic public intellectual who was formerly a Lutheran pastor. As Randy Boyagoda's recent biography of Neuhaus makes clear, Neuhaus was one of the twentieth-century's most important religious thinkers.[17] His book *The Naked Public Square* made a landmark contribution to discussions of religion and public influence, while the journal he founded and edited, *First Things*, was and is the center of learned discussion of matters of public consequence from a theistic perspective. Neuhaus was similar to Colson in some respects: prolific in writing, generous in friendship, ecumenical in temperament.[18]

Colson, Neuhaus, and their ECT associates were not going to take hostility to religion lying down. They recognized they had an opportunity to offer a united witness on the matter of the public square, and they did so. They deserve not only commendation on this point, but emulation. Young evangelicals and Catholics should partner to support the permanent things—life, liberty, and happiness, common grace gifts mediated through the family, the church, and an appropriately bounded society.

Christians should pursue public-square partnership with other religious groups as well. Historic divisions in American public life are crumbling and should crumble. Christians should in no way compromise their doctrine, but should consider making common public-square cause with Jews, Mormons, Muslims, and other religious groups to protect the role of religion in American society. This will not prove an easy or comfortable project, but it is nonetheless one the church should seriously ponder as the culture loses sight of the undeniable good religious groups bring to civil society.

———

In 2015, the coalition of the willing has shrunk drastically from previous years. Fewer people will stand up against injustice and seek to conserve what is virtuous in our society. In years past, Christian leaders could count on a majority of citizens supporting the traditional view of the family or the historic model of marriage. Such a wealth of support has diminished in recent years.

As the Pew Forum has shown, the rise of the "Nones" is a real phenomenon.[19] It will not soon cease. The bottom has dropped out of nominal Christianity in America. A growing number of people no longer see personal benefit in belonging to a church but not attending it. A vibrant religious corps remains (and even thrives), but religion-on-the-fringes is transitioning into no-religion-at-all.

This shift away from a clear religious identity promises to reshape our culture. Our media is growing darker and darker.

The family has been remixed. Fatherlessness is rampant. Divorce is shockingly common and increasingly prominent among older couples. A person's identity as a man or woman is not fixed. The government grows bigger as citizens place more trust in it, their connection to other institutions having weakened. The embrace of homosexuality as not only a viable lifestyle but also even a privileged one is exerting tremendous pressure on young people in particular.

If the culture-norming TV show in the 1980s was *The Cosby Show*, featuring a stable and happy family in the traditional mold, its parallel in our time is *Modern Family*, with the gay couple being the healthiest of all couples shown on the program. Other shows portray the natural family as a problem not a solution, as John Stonestreet of the Colson Center has said.[20]

The center of our modern struggle for the soul of America is human sexuality. Once sex was stewarded, bound to a covenant, exclusive to marriage. Now it is loosed, linked to nothing but desire, guided neither by Scripture nor biology. Nowhere is this more apparent than in sexual relationships, which are increasingly governed by just one word: *consent*. Colleges and universities, for example, actively encourage their students to have sex albeit with this one moralistic maxim: "Yes means yes."[21]

Modern sex is oddly contractual. Two people come together in the heat of the moment. They signal, according to the elaborate process of modern sexual codes, that they want to have sex. But though our age glamorizes sex and elevates it to the point of spirituality, the practice of sex today is individuated. *I get my pleasure; you get yours.* There is no loving oneness, but a separated twoness. Bodily fluids are exchanged, nothing more.

If some mutual interest does develop, the couple enters into a partnership of sorts, an uneasy, ill-defined pseudo-union known as "cohabitation." The writer Tom Wolfe has said of this term that though "nobody under forty had ever heard of the word" in past decades, it is now "the standard form of American court-ship."[22] Cohabitation is in many ways a replacement system for marriage. It is less encumbering and far less stable, making it relatively easy to dissolve. This does not mean there are no consequences to sex, however. There surely are. Enter abortion, which solves the problems that sex creates. Abortion is as much a matter of convenience as it is a matter of principle.

The new sexual ethos unbinds what should be constrained and constrains what should be unbound. It unleashes sexual desire and removes any spiritual considerations from it. On the other hand, it constrains parental love, encouraging couples to abort children produced in the pursuit of hedonistic pleasure. Our modern world leaves us pagans without delight. We feast on the raw pleasures of the body, but without the moral struc-ture and the grand design of the Christian worldview. We are left with the instinct to worship but without a transcendent object. We worship one another instead but find this new reli-gion deeply unsatisfying.

This ethos is full of twists, turns, and contradictions. Perhaps its strangest aspect is its theological nature. Our secular friends rarely reference God more than when they discuss their sexuality: "God made me this way," goes the saying. We most often hear this when people describe either their homosexual tendencies or their transgender inclinations. In such a climate, the church must be clear that the Scripture speaks with one voice about the sinfulness of same-sex desire and behavior.

In our modern culture, the family, the self, and the body

are not fixed realities. They are vanity projects, vehicles for self-expression. Personal identity is now a self-driven project liberated from ethical and theological concerns. Yet our culture is not as secular or atheistic as it thinks. In truth, it is charged with spirituality. It has fallen prey to a peculiar spirituality endemic in our day called *Narcissistic Optimistic Deism*. This is not a formal theological system, but it is alive and well as a general philosophy of life.

I believe this worldview is the successor to what Christian Smith called *Moralistic Therapeutic Deism*. It dispenses with the moralizing instinct and replaces it with the all-consuming self. Its essential confession is this: God lives, but he does not live for his own glory. He lives to give us everything we could ever want. He approves of whatever I do. There is no distinction between sin and holiness; whatever I do is right, because he would not make me imperfect. My body is made not for him, but for my own pleasure. If this sounds like a fusion of self-help thinking, neo-pagan carnality, and man-driven spirituality, I suspect this is because it is. The self is the center of all things; sexuality is our chief mode of expression. The body has no script; manhood and womanhood do not *mean* anything. The body is given us to gratify our lusts, and gratification brings holistic satisfaction.

The church must be crystal clear on this point: our identity is not inherently sexual. We are not the sum of our lusts, our perversity, our fallenness, whatever shape such sin takes, whether heterosexual, homosexual, or any other form. We will not find happiness and freedom when we allow our lusts free reign. We will only thrive when our sexuality is kept under control, and there is no force more powerful than the Holy Spirit.

None of this means that sex is problematic for Christians.

God, not *Maxim* or *50 Shades of Grey*, invented sex. It is a good gift and a source of delight when it is ordered according to God's design. But even for married couples, sex is only a part of our lives, and in many cases, it's a small part. You would not know that from movies, television shows, and pop music. Our sexualized culture tempts us to make sex the most important part of our beings. But whether we're single or married, this frankly is not so. We are each an image-bearer; we are each a man or a woman; if redeemed, the single most important truth about us is that we are in Christ and will be into all eternity and beyond.

We are not only sexual beings. We are intellectual, moral, spiritual, emotional, and psychological beings. We each have a soul, a body, and a mind. We are unified beings, but composed of many parts. Sexuality is one of them. We must make this clear to people who are encouraged to make any sexual interest their identity. This is a relevant matter. Today, the culture exhorts us to affirm that homosexual identity and same-sex marriage are inherently good. The Bible, however, presents homosexual activity of any kind as sinful (Gen. 19; Lev. 18:22; Deut. 23:17–18; Rom. 1:26–27; 1 Cor. 6:9; 1 Tim. 1:10).[23] We cannot approve of it.

We cannot tell people embracing such an identity that they are in good standing with God and in a position to flourish. Gender dysphoria and sexual confusion are real. In some cases, they are the result of abuse and neglect. The church exists to hold out compassion for people who are victims. We know, of all people, how cruel this world is, and yet how kind and welcoming our Savior is. The solution to sin, whether our own or that inflicted upon us, is never found in ourselves, however. Only God's truth will heal our brokenness. Though abuse victims have done nothing to merit such evil treatment, we must also communicate that every one of us has fallen in Adam (Rom. 3:10–18). We cannot respond to brokenness by embracing it and its effects. We will find freedom only in the transforming gospel of Jesus Christ.

It is also the church's glad responsibility to stand for the goodness of the body. Manhood and womanhood are not incidental aspects of our beings, as is now commonly taught. We do not have bodies but choose our genders. We are each either a man or a woman, a boy or a girl. We must all inhabit our manhood or womanhood; one thinks of David saying to Solomon, "Show yourself a man," for example (1 Kings 2:2). Our identities as men or women is not a problem to solve. We have been given our bodies as gifts. They tell us who we are and what we are to be. We are not all the same; men and women share much as bearers of God's image, but we are also constituted differently to the glory of God. Simply standing for these basic truths may bring profound criticism and even persecution to the church, but we cannot say otherwise.[24]

The church has the opportunity to re-enchant the world. Though many young people today have grown up in a cynical, broken world, they are hungry for truth, beauty, and goodness. They want to believe in these things. They sense that light is stronger than darkness, and though they find themselves in a changing and confusing age, they do not want to give in to despair. They are sinners as every person is, but they sense that there is something greater than the self, better than raw sex, and more meaningful than a man-made God.

Today, we find ourselves in a contest of narratives. In a very real sense, our society increasingly takes the form of a great cultural debate between the coalition of the religious and the proponents of secularism. In historical terms, we could reduce the debate to these terms: America is caught between allegiance to the First Great Awakening and allegiance to the Enlightenment.[25] These competitors coexisted and even co-operated in this country for common ends for many decades. But now the uneasy synthesis of worldviews is pulling apart. With this fragmentation comes a competition of visions: Whose pleasure is better? Whose conception of humanity is fulfilling? Whose understanding of the self is superior?

As is clear, Christians are not simply haggling over moral niceties with our secular friends. We have the chance to show our neighbors that God has created us. Life with Jesus is what our hearts naturally seek. We possess God-given worth as men and women. He has designed and created us for pleasure in his name. The body is not a script to rewrite, but a gift to inhabit. Sex is not made for its own sake, but for the union of a couple and the imaging of love, even divine love. God becomes our friend through faith in Christ and his work on the cross, but he is equally our Lord, our Ruler, and the one we owe obedience and worship. He does not exist for us. We were made for him.

The church can grow cranky and despairing in our secu-larizing age. It can lose itself in a gloomy forecast of the future. Or it can understand the times and work afresh to bring hope to people deadened by sin and disillusioned by the world's bro-ken promises. We love our neighbors; we want them to flourish. People who disagree with us, even strenuously, are not our oppo-nents. We are doing battle with far greater forces, forces that would undo us (Eph. 6:12).

That is why we walk into the public square with all its com-motion and chaos. We have a challenge, but more than this, we have an opportunity to make the case for gospel flourishing.

This was the way Chuck Colson looked at a fallen world and a compromised society. He analyzed it, scrutinizing its flaws and devastation. But he did so to figure out how to minister to it, not rail at it. He was a venture capitalist for hope. That, and not condemnation, was ultimately what he offered his neighbor.

A CHRISTIAN WORLDVIEW

This effort paid off in serious ways. By the mid-1990s, Colson had created a panoply of projects: Prison Fellowship and Prison Fellowship International, Angel Tree, the Wilberforce Forum, ECT, and *BreakPoint*. In this period, Colson gave special attention to ideas. He devoted himself to the promotion of Christian worldview thinking. Colson was not the only figure in the 1980s and 1990s to become prominent in this field; Schaeffer, James Sire, Josh McDowell, Os Guinness, and a number of others labored profitably as worldview experts.

It was Colson who popularized the discipline, making it a household term in tens of thousands of homes and churches in this period and beyond. *BreakPoint* played on hundreds and eventually thousands of stations all across America, supplementing the prodigious sales of Colson's books (more than five million total, by one 2008 count).[26]

Chuck Colson created many initiatives. Some might thus find it curious that he never founded a college or university. The program that began as the Wilberforce Fellowship and morphed into the Centurions represents his attempt to educate the next generation. By any measure, the Centurions (still operative) have helped to pass on the essential perspective and ideas of Colson as a worldview proponent. In 2015, the program has commissioned one thousand Centurions, including Gabe Lyons of Q Ideas, Kelli Mutz of PricewaterhouseCoopers, and Everett Piper, president of Oklahoma Wesleyan University. These and many other young Christians have received training resulting in "inward formation for outward action," a phrase that nicely sums up the reflective Colson's central concern.[27]

Colson supported many evangelical schools. He spoke regularly at institutions like Wheaton College, Trinity Evangelical Divinity School, and Union University (and accrued fifteen honorary doctorates along the way). He gave lectures at countless secular institutions including Harvard, Yale, Princeton, and Brown. Though he was never a tenured chair at a university, Colson was essentially a professor-at-large to evangelicalism. His chosen discipline was a blend of worldview and apologetics, what we could call philosophy at the ground level. As the preceding material has shown, Colson deserves recognition as a leading Christian public intellectual of the period.

Over the years, Colson influenced many future Christian leaders. One who heard Colson's broadcasts, read his books, and studied his model as a statesman is R. Albert Mohler, Jr., the president of the Southern Baptist Theological Seminary. Mohler first encountered Colson while a young man. "My introduction to Chuck Colson came in two ways: one was as a teenager. I was aware of him as a public figure as my early teen years coincided with the Watergate scandal." Like many evangelicals, Mohler was effectively reintroduced to Colson after the fallen leader came to faith. "His conversion to Christ and publication of the book *Born Again* came as I was in high school. His example had a tremendous encouraging effect on me. Here was a man, after all, who had been in the middle of the biggest political scandal in American history."[28]

When Colson declared his newfound faith, "many people feared that this was a typical sad celebrity conversion, that it was more ephemeral than real," Mohler remembered. But the young man saw even then that he "had deep theological content. His ministry had a deep resonance with Christian truth and exhibited a transformative encounter with that truth."

As Colson's ministry deepened over the years, Mohler learned from his interaction with ideas. "Chuck was one of the first American evangelical leaders to make the emphatic point that cultural engagement required Christian leaders to speak to what the culture was most concerned about at the time." As Mohler understood him, "Colson was concerned that Christians tended to wait to respond to issues until they could write a book." Colson, by contrast, practiced what Mohler called "modern pamphleteering. He knew that a response needed to be given right now, while the conversation was taking place."

This example had a profound effect on Mohler, who began his own media ministry, which now includes articles on major cultural and theological debates, a podcast, and appearances on numerous TV shows. The instruction Colson afforded Mohler paid off. The young theologian and seminary president was named "evangelicalism's reigning public intellectual" in 2003 by *TIME* magazine.[29]

The example is illustrative of a broader trend in Colson's life. Though he never became a full-time professor on a college campus, he ministered to many students. He engaged the great contest of ideas and influenced untold evangelicals both by his own analyses and his model. The model mattered greatly to young Christians like Mohler. Here was an urbane, sophisticated, and gracious spokesman for gospel truth. Colson was as comfortable speaking to fellow Ivy Leaguers and kingmakers as he was his Sunday school class.

In a period of increasing secularization, Colson's comportment and zest for intellectual engagement made him an appealing figure to emerging Christians hungry for leadership. Radio show host Erick Erickson echoed Mohler in his assessment of Colson's ministry: "He went where the needs were. He reached out to where people were in life. I use Colson as an example."[30] Erickson was impressed by Colson's willingness to labor where the need was great. "Good Christian churches send their kids on glorified mission trips," Erickson said, "and meanwhile you have a collapsing inner city. The Chuck Colsons of the world go there rather than to the beach."

Matthew Schmitz, the young deputy editor of *First Things*, spoke to how Colson influenced him as a practitioner. "He exemplified a committed intelligence," a personal quality on display when Colson spoke at Princeton University during Schmitz's student days. Colson showed Schmitz that one could be both "smart and sophisticated yet committed to advocating for truth. He was probably the first model I had for Christian public engagement."[31] This was valuable at Princeton University, which offered few personal examples of richly intellectual faith.

Colson's example reminds us of the profound need in our day to provide a gospel witness on the campuses of American colleges and universities. This is not an easy task, and it is growing more challenging in 2015. In past years, schools like Tufts University, Bowdoin College, the California State University campuses, and others have "derecognized" on-campus evangelical groups affiliated with InterVarsity Christian Fellowship and Cru. This is noteworthy, for secularism has long promised it would usher in the age of tolerance. It seems in some places, however, to have rendered evangelical groups unfit to be tolerated.

Campus ministry is a vital form of Christian outreach. We are encouraged by Colson's engagement with ideas to do all we can today to continue ministering the gospel to college students. This will likely increasingly mean that churches must partner with other organizations. The Christian Study Center movement is one of the most promising developments along these lines.[32] Where possible, centers buy a house or facility near a campus and invite students to come for Bible study, discipleship, and intellectual training. Programs of this kind function best when they are strongly connected to a local church where students can become members. The church also needs to support both evangelical professors and students who can withstand the serious pressure of such environments, and who can serve as witnesses in them.

THE TEMPLETON PRIZE

Colson thrilled to make the case for Christianity to skeptical audiences. His efforts attracted international attention in the early 1990s. In 1993, he won the world's most prestigious award for religious work, the Templeton Prize. The award is given to a person who "has made an exceptional contribution to affirming life's spiritual dimension." The recipient wins more than $1 million and is thus recognized as a world leader in religious work in a splashy ceremony at Buckingham Palace in London.

The Templeton Prize website recognizes Colson as the

founder of Prison Fellowship, "now the largest prison outreach program in the world, operating a network of ministries in more than 110 nations. The organization has made substantial gains in breaking the cycle of crime and recidivism."[33] The list of Templeton honorees is impressive: Billy Graham won in 1982, Alexander Solzhenitsyn in 1983. In more recent years, scientist John Polkinghorne won in 2002 and Charles Taylor, renowned critic of secularism, won in 2007.

Colson traveled to England to receive the award in March 1993 and promptly donated the entire prize to Prison Fellowship. This was not unusual for Colson. He could have made millions for himself through his books, speeches, and media, but he chose to donate nearly every penny he earned to Prison Fellowship. In September 1993, Colson gave the Templeton Address at the University of Chicago. The address, as much as any other, exemplifies what Colson championed in his public-square witness.

"The Enduring Revolution," as it was titled, initially outlined why Christian engagement was essential. Humanity faced "four horsemen of the present apocalypse," as Colson put it. These were four great "myths," in his view, that bewitched people and deceived them. The first, "the goodness of man," tricked "people into thinking that they are always victims, never villains; always deprived, never depraved." The second horseman Colson identified was "the promise of coming utopia." The third horseman was the "relativity of moral values." Here Colson rightly saw the individualist trajectory of the postmodern world. "When a society abandons its transcendent values," he argued, "each individual's moral vision becomes purely personal and finally equal." Once the ground was cleared, the fourth horseman, "radical individualism," entered the picture. "This myth dismisses the importance of family, church, and community; denies the value of sacrifice; and elevates individual rights and pleasures as the ultimate social value."

Chuck Colson watched these trends and did not stay quiet. In "The Enduring Revolution," he proclaimed that Christian conviction had not died. It lived, and it was primed to foster public virtue.[34] Colson wanted Christ to be lifted high: "by the Cross He offers hope" and "by the Resurrection He assures His triumph."[35] This was no "out there" righteousness for Colson. It was not an abstraction. This revolution begins in the human heart. Speaking directly to the Templeton Foundation, Colson noted that this was the progress in religion that mankind needed. The world seemed hopeless by some accounts, but Christ and his invincible kingdom "reaches into the darkest corners of every community" and "into the darkest corners of every mind."[36]

In the midst of this darkness, Colson saw abundant reason for hope. He was far too grounded to be blithely optimistic. He was also much too biblically minded to plummet into despair. He practiced what we could call *Christocentric realism*. As he made clear in London, Colson found solace and optimism not in political takeover, but in the "Cross of Christ" and the "enduring revolution" it created. His goal was not to "take America back" from its foes. Chuck Colson wanted the fame of Jesus to spread. That was where he banked his hope as a born-again believer.

In his Templeton address, Colson identified two major threats: unfettered individualism and a Messianic state. Each still looms large as a problem in 2015. We are a nation of individuals, a collective of the isolated. Our individuation is not benign, however. Our self-entitlement represents a threat to the social order. Alongside the regnant individual is the unencumbered state, which promises to solve our problems and standardize our lives. It is a strange mix, to be sure. Yet these trends are carving out a new moral and social order in our time. The church witnesses these shifts and is disturbed by them. It does not often know, however, how to respond. It feels, in fact, like the best thing to do is simply to stay quiet and hope for the best. But this is not best. Christians need to recover a sense of agency in such days, one that operates out of a desire to spread flourishing and love our neighbor.

Our activism is twofold. We must promote the good where it has not taken root on the one hand and hold fast to existing virtue on the other. Progressives understand the first part. They feel the fervor of the French Revolution in their bones. They want to remake the world. To an extent, evangelicals do as well. We want to be light, as Jesus said. But we also want to preserve the virtuous. We want to be salt as well. We do not choose one or the other. We bring light into all the rooms we can enter. We act as salt in every place we can.

In this sense, Christians are the true progressives. We believe in conserving and promoting the good in order that future generations can flourish. We do not believe the future lies in demolishing the past. We believe the future is brightest when the wisdom of the past is handed down. It is of course true that not everything about the past is good. Christians, to our shame, have historically been on the wrong side of some social debates. Women have not enjoyed the freedom they should have, despite the way Jesus enfranchises women as full citizens of his kingdom. A good number of American evangelicals supported slavery, to our everlasting shame. If we reach back in history to events like the Crusades, we see an unholy alliance of church and state that Christians cannot scripturally support.

Young Christians can be honest about these failings. Our doctrine of sin comprehends all of life as under the sway of depravity. Yet though our past is not pure, Christians historically have been a force for social good. We have opposed social and cultural evil over the ages, offering a sacrificial witness unto life. The Christian moral tradition is rich and multitextured. The early church saved the lives of babies who were left to die in the cold night air by the pagan Greeks. Telemachus, a young monk, shut down the horrific gladiator games in the fifth century. When Christians stayed to care for the sick in times of plague, they showed the world that they did not fear death and were willing to risk their lives to care for the needy. Many evangelicals campaigned zealously against slavery in Europe and America.[37]

These and other acts of courage show that evangelicals are a kingdom people with protest instincts. Our primary purpose is to proclaim the existence of a hidden kingdom, one that offers humanity all it could ever want: justice, righteousness, grace, and hope. For this reason the church exists: to proclaim the good news of this kingdom ruled by a slain but risen Messiah. But we are also well versed in protest. We do not only speak positively what should be; we also decry what is wrong. We speak up on behalf of all who are wronged. This includes ourselves.

Some young evangelicals feel hesitant about defending themselves. They think we imperil our witness by bothering to speak on our behalf. Jesus, after all, went to the cross. He did not defend himself. I understand this line of thinking, and if we are called to die for our faith, we should be ready to die. As long as we have cultural agency and the ability to protest evil, we should. We are reminded of how the apostle Paul appealed to the Roman authorities on the basis of his status as a Roman citizen. He did not lay down any argument once apprehended for preaching the gospel. He defended himself. Christians do not often consider the following passage. It is crucial for understanding how we conduct ourselves when wronged:

> But when they had stretched him out for the whips, Paul said to the centurion who was standing by, "Is it lawful for you to flog a man who is a Roman citizen and uncondemned?" When the centurion heard this, he went to the tribune and said to him, "What are you about to do? For this man is a Roman citizen." So the tribune came and said to him, "Tell me, are you a Roman citizen?" And he said, "Yes." The tribune answered, "I bought this citizenship for a large sum." Paul said, "But I am a citizen by birth." So those who were about to examine him withdrew from him immediately, and the tribune also was afraid, for he realized that Paul was a Roman citizen and that he had bound him. (Acts 22:25–29)

If a person strikes us for our faith, we should not avenge the blow. We should turn the other cheek (Matt. 5:39). But as Paul's example shows us, we need not submit to unjust persecution. When wrongs are committed against the church, we should not take them lying down. We should raise our voices. We should speak up. We should do the same when wrongs are committed against our neighbors.

Our primary calling in the world is to collectively fulfill the Great Commission (Matt. 28:16–20). But we also exist to decry evil when no one else will speak. We have seen that God called Moses to his prophetic ministry to stand down Pharaoh (Ex. 9).

We have read the account of Daniel defiantly refusing to abide by pagan standards (Dan. 1). We have heard about the murder of John the Baptist because of his refusal to tolerate illicit sexuality (Matt. 14:1–12). We know, furthermore, that if we do not speak up, fewer and fewer will. In America, we still have a great deal of cultural agency. We should use it. We would be unwise stewards if we failed to do so.

None of this means that we should clothe ourselves in sack-cloth. We live in hope. We are a people who have seen and tasted that hope is real. It is not an impersonal force; it is a person, Jesus Christ. With this foundation, we believe that the future can be bright. We see that though much has been lost, much has been preserved. In all our cultural engagement and political involvement, we promote the good and defend the virtuous, believing that God can work in days ahead as he did in days past.

This was true of Chuck Colson. He brimmed with optimism. He could not stop working. As Michael Cromartie observed, "He thought like a Calvinist but worked like an Arminian." He was also constantly asked to write more books, give more speeches, and endorse more causes than was possible for any one person. One project he had great enthusiasm for was a PBS documentary called "Searching for God in America." The host was Hugh Hewitt, a conservative Renaissance man who is known today as one of America's preeminent media voices. Hewitt recounted in an interview how he brought Colson in the show: "After the 1994 election, I got an offer from PBS to host the show. The first name out of my mouth was Chuck Colson. I wanted to open the series with a faithful presentation of traditional Christianity."[38]

Colson came ready to preach when he talked with Hewitt on camera. When Colson taped his portion of the program, Hewitt remembered, he "knew exactly what he wanted to accomplish: preaching the gospel." Colson was then at "the top of his game." They spent two hours taping, and Colson "said the same thing over and over again. He was there to preach Christ crucified, risen, and reigning at the right hand of God." Colson knew how media interviews worked, and he repeated the gospel message in simple terms so that it could not be avoided in the post-production room. Hewitt, of course, had no such intention. He knew what Colson's heartbeat was: "He never missed a chance to preach the gospel."

He preached it everywhere he could. Throughout the 1990s, he continued his nonstop program of speaking, touring, and writing. His book *How Now Shall We Live?* made waves in 1998, becoming one of his bestselling works. The text, written with gifted apologist Nancy Pearcey, a longtime *BreakPoint* editor, called for a bold approach to the decline of the West and the ailments of the church. The real issue was not a culture war of a bipartisan kind, but a spiritual battle. "[W]e've been fighting cultural skirmishes on all sides without knowing what the war itself is about," the authors said. They wanted their audience to see that "the real war is a cosmic struggle between worldviews—between the Christian worldview and the various secular and spiritual worldviews arrayed against it."

The mission of the book was to help the church "be effective in evangelizing our world today and in transforming it to reflect the wisdom of the Creator."[39] By exploring stories and ideas related to this theme, the authors sketched a plan by which Christians could plunge into their surroundings to bring hope to them. Colson and Pearcey sought a spiritual and intellectual awakening of the church. As Francis Schaeffer had done in his video series *How Then Shall We Live?*, they argued that Christianity was both intellectually and personally true.

Like Schaeffer, the authors wanted to see Christians push beyond partisan bickering and understand that "Christianity is an accurate road map of reality," and that as such, believers should "be ready to make the case to those who are growing increasingly aware of the futility of all other worldviews."[40] They asked, *"How now shall we live?"* and answered as follows: "By embracing God's truth, understanding the physical and moral order he has created, lovingly contending for that truth with our neighbors, then having the courage to live it out in every walk of life. Boldly and, yes, joyously."[41]

Colson persisted in this outlook as he led Prison Fellowship and continued expanding its work. In 2000, Colson showed his interest in tackling new social evils. He worked with Virginia Republican congressman Frank Wolf to fight sex trafficking. Colson remembered Wolf's bravery years later: "Frank was one of the first people to speak out on this issue, and he was absolutely relentless against the fierce opposition of the Clinton administration, which wanted to help women find 'work' by allowing certain prostitution rings to flourish."[42] United in a common cause, the two men became fast friends. "Chuck was a Marine—hard-headed, tough, understood the political process very well, but then he had the faith component. Very few leaders I meet have that combination."[43]

Wolf regularly accessed Colson's wisdom as he sought to craft legislation that would minister to the forgotten and needy of society. "He was a bright guy, a deep thinker," Wolf later said, "and so I would call him about once a month to ask him, 'What do you think?'" Colson also propelled Wolf not only to advocate for those in dire straits, but to visit them: "He went to the least of the least, and they understood him, and he understood them."

INNERCHANGE

Colson never stopped visiting prisoners and seeking new ways to bring them the gospel. Other initiatives drew Colson's attention during this period. The InnerChange Freedom Initiative, a program started in Brazil and championed by Prison Fellowship, drew a huge amount of media coverage because of its focus on evangelism in federal prisons. InnerChange sought to provide stable and spiritually guided "reentry" into society to prisoners who had finished their jail sentences. It was "based on the life and teachings of Jesus Christ." In 2003, President George W. Bush backed the initiative, lending his support through the White House's Office of Faith-Based Initiatives. When governor of Texas in 1997, Bush had opened the doors of state prisons to InnerChange, and his support was deep and well documented.[44]

His backing was also strongly opposed. In the article "Chuck Colson's Jails for Jesus," Samantha Shapiro of *Mother Jones* asserted that InnerChange offered little more than preferential treatment for inmates who attended it. The program trained inmates to proselytize, a dubious practice, and Colson and his staffers went so far as to believe that Christianity could better society, a conviction that unsettled Shapiro: "Bush's faith-based initiatives promote a very different theology of social action— one that he and Colson have personally experienced—that claims religion itself is the cure for social ills." Colson's activist instincts put him in direct tension with a secular society. He could not stop working, however. He believed with absolute certainty that Christianity would benefit both the individual and the society, whereas secularism would ultimately produce only suffering on both accounts.

The worst fears of *Mother Jones* were realized. Chuck Colson was a true-blue evangelical who thought the only lasting hope for America was the gospel and its ethic. Worse, Colson dared to act on his principles. Where some Christians sat back and marveled at their country's lost condition, Colson plunged into it, breaking through barriers, upsetting secularized onlookers, showing no regard for walls between faith and society he considered artificial.

The question is not an easy one to answer. Colson and the ministry he led, however, were glad to be given the chance to do ministry in prisons. They were only able to do so because numerous states wanted Prison Fellowship to engage their inmates. The program had a strong track record, it was led by a prisoner wholly transformed by Christian doctrine, and many state leaders genuinely wanted inmates to become productive citizens. It was true that IFI taught an explicitly Christian program. But it did so at the pleasure of lawmakers and leaders who saw value in it. IFI was not a theocratic takeover of the American incarceration system. It never took federal funds, it drew funding from states for only a limited time, and it served—with considerable success—at the invitation of those who desired the full flourishing of struggling prisoners.

Evangelicals who share Colson's desire to see prisoners saved and transformed by the gospel would no doubt applaud a no-holds-barred approach. Rather than try and reason out every moral implication of a program like InnerChange or wring his hands over whether federal funding meant that Hindu and Bahai groups could now evangelize on the government's dime, Colson showed a willingness to tap the system's resources for good.

A big thinker, Colson was not content with a small prospectus. His conception of God fit with his conception of life. God was great, and he allowed even finite and frail creatures to undertake great things in his name. This was the kind of existence Colson hungered after. He dreamed big dreams. He crafted big, almost impossible, goals. He did not fulfill all of them, and those he did meet he met imperfectly. But one could not fault Colson for expecting great things of God and attempting great things for God.

We face the same challenge today. We're tempted to privatize our faith, to lock it away in a little heart-shaped box. We're told that religion and worship are perfectly acceptable so long as we don't bring our convictions into the public arena. Faith is fine for spiritual moments we cherish in the comfortable confines of our own quiet piety. It is increasingly less acceptable in the public square, in the arena where ideas are exchanged and principles are debated. Chuck Colson sensed this standard and defied it. He refused to lock his faith away. He could not abide failing to live by his beliefs.

We must not privatize our convictions. We need to out our faith in the rough-and-tumble of a fallen world. Let us make this as plain as we can: more young evangelicals, many more, need to get plugged in to the momentous public-square issues of the day. But they need to do so with an eye toward staying in the game. It took decades for Wilberforce to see the realization of his abolitionist advocacy. Where is his successor, male or female, on the matter of abortion? Who will dedicate his or her entire life to the eradication of this horror? Who cares about the natural family, and the constellation of blessings it brings, enough to make this cause his or her lodestar and never waver in promoting it?

Who will speak up for religious liberty, taking hit after hit for his or her stance, so that American religious groups do not lose their voice and their right to live according to their consciences? Will any of these issues—and others like sex trafficking and racial unity—hold the attention of young Christians longer than a football game or a movie? Beyond just one person or a handful of such advocates, will an entire generation rise up in love of neighbor and not rest until abortion is outlawed in America?

Every Christian can contribute to these great causes. Whether working in the Beltway, driving through New England hills to work, or raising children in Orange County, young evangelicals can engage the struggle from their own vantage points. This may mean prayer; it may mean speaking up on social media; it may mean training a church to develop a robust doctrine of loving your neighbor that goes beyond mere cookie baking; it may even mean moving to the corridors of power and devoting one's life to influencing them in a God-glorifying direction. All these roles can be filled for God. All this work can be done unto God.

Martin Luther once counseled a church member to "sin boldly." He meant by this not that his parishioners should transgress God's commands with impunity, as it might sound, but that their fearfulness of overstepping the bounds of propriety should not so constrain them that they feared to act in God's name. Colson knew that he was not perfect. He could not hold back from acting, though, because a failure to act constituted a failure to witness. He would break the china, even when no one else was willing.

His training under Chesty Puller introduced him to the necessity of fearlessness. In the political ring, he could take a punch, and he could throw one. As a speaker at his 2012 memorial service noted, on an airplane flight he told a fellow passenger who antagonized him, "Fellow, do you know who you are messing with here? I'm an ex-Marine, ex-con, and if I wasn't a Christian, you'd be ON THE FLOOR." He then shared Christ with the man.[45]

Colson was unafraid. The worst had happened to him. Because of Watergate he lost his career, his prestige, and his winning streak. He went to prison and was pilloried by a press that strongly disliked him. What could have been a tragedy and left him broken instead gave him a spine of steel. He needed it. In 2002, he drew fire for joining a group of religious leaders led by Southern Baptist Richard Land who called for early intervention in Iraq against Saddam Hussein, who was then gassing his people and constructing frightening weapons.

Colson continued to tackle a range of controversial topics on *BreakPoint*. The show was hosted on more than fourteen hundred stations by 2010. He wrote op-eds on a continual basis for *Christianity Today*, writing the column "Contra Mundum" for a number of years with Timothy George. Though he did not agree with President Barack Obama's political views, he called the church in 2008 to look to God for hope. "This," he said in *The Sky Is Not Falling*, a collection of *Christianity Today* columns, "is the worst possible time for Christians to despair." Instead, "This is the time to make a compelling case that Christianity offers the only rational and realistic hope for both personal redemption and social renewal."[46]

As his career came to a close, Colson made the case for a socially engaged faith. He believed that his fellow evangelicals were in danger of abandoning it. "Chuck was very concerned about the loss of a public vision," George later recalled. "We traveled a good bit together, and so we would speak together. It was not a secret, his concern that the Christian faith not be reduced to a Pietistic 'Jesus in my heart' kind of approach on the one hand, and that it not lose the 'gospel speaking into the culture' approach."[47]

THE MANHATTAN DECLARATION

The Manhattan Declaration, written in 2009, represents Colson's final major public effort to apply the gospel to the culture. Published in 2009 after a meeting in midtown Manhattan of nearly two hundred leaders from across the spectrum of Christian denominations, the declaration was a direct response to the spirit of the times and a clarion call to the church to speak life to a secular culture. Robert P. George, McCormick Chair in Jurisprudence at Princeton University and one of the drafters of the Declaration, later observed that Colson had long sought to "transcend historic differences of Nicene Christianity." He wanted "a forum for the common witness of the essential truths of the Christian faith shared by Eastern Orthodoxy, evangelicalism, and Catholicism. This included not only Christological and theological dogmas but also the central moral teachings of the human faith."[48]

George shared that Colson held a dim view of the American political scene. "Chuck saw the tsunami coming, knowing how political power is used and abused. Now the left has consolidated its power. This means an unprecedented assault on the principles we believe are at the foundation of our polity, civic order, and even our faith." The Princeton professor noted that Colson was unusually aware of the ramifications of this trend. "He foresaw it all," George remembered. "He said we need to unite the Christian community, beginning with leadership, in defense of these principles and to pledge that we will not yield to the demand that we implicate ourselves in the wrongdoing that will be promoted and backed by political power."

From this fundamental conviction came the impetus to write the Manhattan Declaration. By 2009, Colson had convening power second only to Billy Graham. He called for a gathering of Christian leaders in New York City that would feature several talks addressing the fractured public square and the need for a reinvigorated and united Christian witness. In September 2009, more than one hundred leaders gathered at the Union League Club for meetings. From this gathering, in November 2009, a document was produced that was called "The Manhattan Declaration: A Call of Christian Conscience." The document's name was intended to evoke the Barmen Declaration of the Confessing Church in Nazi Germany. The document focused on three key matters, which the authors expressed as affirmations:

> Because the sanctity of human life, the dignity of marriage as a union of husband and wife, and the freedom of conscience and religion are foundational principles of justice and the common good, we are compelled by our Christian faith to speak and act in their defense. In this declaration we affirm: 1) the profound, inherent, and equal dignity of every human being as a creature fashioned in the very image of God, possessing inherent rights of equal dignity and life; 2) marriage as

a conjugal union of man and woman, ordained by God from the creation, and historically understood by believers and non-believers alike, to be the most basic institution in society and; 3) religious liberty, which is grounded in the character of God, the example of Christ, and the inherent freedom and dignity of human beings created in the divine image.

Colson wanted to invite not only key signatories to affix their names to the Manhattan Declaration (ManDec) but also "Christians from all walks of life." He was a consummate populist. The man who had convinced organized labor to vote in droves for Nixon was not about to write his life's manifesto and have it vanish in the next day's media cycle. "So we created the site with mechanisms to sign," George said. Hundreds of thousands did. As of this writing, ManDec has more than 550,000 signatures.

Colson thrilled to see this groundswell of support. George noted that "[Colson] regarded this as his legacy. There were many things he had done and built but this was a witness to the foundational principles of faith and polity. That would be his true and greatest legacy." Colson said as much to the *New York Times* in November 2009 when the document was released.

"We argue that there is a hierarchy of issues," said Charles Colson, a prominent evangelical who founded Prison Fellowship after serving time in prison for his role in the Watergate scandal. "A lot of the younger evangelicals say they're all alike. We're hoping to educate them that these are the three most important issues."[49]

This was a strong statement to make to young evangelicals.

ManDec, as Colson made clear, was not only a manifesto. It was a statement of priority for the next generation.

In 2014, years after the document's writing, George, the Princeton professor, reflected on Colson's motivations. The marriage of Colson's faith and his patriotism impelled him to act, George argued: "He was a marine. He believed in the country. The principles of the American founding were fundamentally good. Of course, he was conscious of our country's past acceptance of slavery and Jim Crow laws. He wasn't some rose-colored-glasses-wearing patriot." Though Colson was self-aware in his patriotism, "he did think our fundamental principles were sound, and that if you tally up the whole record, the U.S. has been much more a force for good, a force for liberation from tyranny—one thinks of World War II and the twilight struggle against Communism."[50]

America's close connection to Christianity was a key part of this heritage, according to George. "The two—faith and the American founding—were compatible. Consequently, Christians should fight to uphold those principles." George's words speak to the defining work of Chuck Colson's later years, a period capped off by the Manhattan Declaration. The burden of his work shows the conviction of his heart: that Christians must speak and act in the name of the Lord Jesus Christ.

ManDec was oriented around this conviction, and it became a formal organization in 2010 after the statement went viral, attracting more than 500,000 signatures. Eric Teetsel, a young evangelical who graduated from Wheaton College, was soon chosen to be the executive director. He was deeply affected by Colson's legacy: "His story gives me hope that I too can be of use to a God who yearns to forgive and redeem fallen men." In 2015, ManDec's work continues, led courageously by Teetsel.

The causes championed by Colson live on. His ministry endures and continues to inspire the church to speak and to act in the name of Christ. Colson loved the cut-and-thrust of public-square debate, but by the final years of his life he saw, as few did, that the church's social prospects were in jeopardy. Colson saw himself as a witness. Engaging Saab advertisements or death-row prisoners called forth the same instinct in Colson: to never give up the life of a witness. He was called to this role. He could not leave it.

In the end, there was only one factor that could bring Colson's work as a witness to a close: the final foe, death.

SEVEN

TWILIGHT

Chuck Colson splashed his arms into the water. He was a sea monster. One of the most serious-minded people in all America had morphed into a fearsome aquatic beast. The monster would consume anything in his path, but he had a special interest in finding one particular creature: his grandson Max. Max shrieked with delight as the now-elderly Colson made a loud sea-monster noise. As Emily Colson later remembered it, "Max laughed as he shot out of the water like a geyser."[1]

It is quite clear to the student of Colson's life that he made the most of the time given him by God. Emily, in fact, remembered that over the years, her ever-dynamic father would schedule Colson family vacations so closely that, after a series of energetic activities, coordinated meals, and tightly managed family inter-actions, he would look at his watch and say, "All right everybody, take five minutes and just rest."[2] Colson, to put it mildly, did not excel at relaxation.

But something changed in Colson when his autistic grandson Max came into the picture. Early on with Max, Colson thought, *I'm not wired for this.* Children of any kind challenge an innate sense of control, bringing us into confrontation with our selfishness. As time developed, Colson warmed to the task. "I've grown to love becoming an ordinary grandfather. When Emily and Max come," he noted, "I clear the decks. No writing, no *BreakPoint* broadcast recordings, no answering calls."[3]

For Max's part, visits yielded an explosion of joy. "Grandpa! Grandpa! Happy! Happy!" Max would shout, finding Chuck and Patty in the airport. Once on the ground, Max was all business. Emily recorded his "Florida To Do" list in her book *Dancing with Max*:

1. Visit Publix grocery store
2. See the refrigerators at CVS pharmacy
3. Drive on specific highways and take photographs of street signs, bridges, and traffic lights

The grandfather prosecuted Max's to-do list as only Colson could, roaming the aisles of Publix for long spells, soberly inspecting CVS coolers, and traveling back and forth (many times) over different bridges and streets that caught Max's attention. It is clear that Chuck Colson entered fully into his grandson's world. His grandson, in return, did not hold back in loving him. He saw Colson, a man who became a target and object of slander for many, as a rock. To visit Grandpa was to enter into something close to bliss itself.

In this little profile of Colson the grandfather, we see his caring, attentive side. This aspect of Colson his family was most able to see. But we also see how Colson treated all people with dignity. He was not only a passionate man but also a deeply compassionate one. Though he certainly did not assume the persona of sea monster for a wide audience, he was a tireless advocate for those who had little voice, little influence, in society. He filled this role until the end of his life.

———

When he was not a sea monster, Colson was presiding in his later years over an expansive ministry empire. By 2008, Prison Fellowship's budget was more than $50 million. Its efforts reached across the world and across platforms. As former Colson Center for Christian Worldview president Alan Terwilliger later remembered, Colson had long ago decided that he needed to give attention to "key issues upstream" in American culture "that were the reason we had all these downstream issues," including crime, community breakdown, and sky-high incarceration rates. "Life, marriage, religious liberty, and the free market needed to be addressed and understood" such that "you'd have less government and cause for dysfunction."

Like any great leader, Colson had not merely recruited employees and financial backers. He cast all their labor on behalf of prisoners and the broader society as a "movement," a cause that sought greater influence than any one program could wield. Colson and his "unit" wanted to change the culture. As of 2011, Jim Liske would lead Prison Fellowship in this regard. It was never easy for Colson to fill positions within Prison Fellowship, for they required a specific skill set and passion for a ministry that was at once focused and broad. Years earlier, Colson had offered the position to Mark Dever, pastor of Capitol Hill Baptist Church, Washington, DC. A Cambridge PhD and a sterling preacher, Dever sensed a call to keep pastoring CHBC, despite Colson's prodigious and flattering efforts.[4]

In this last chapter of his life, Colson was slowing. He did not slow down much, however. He continued to develop and raise up new leaders. Colson was an encourager and reached out regularly to young evangelicals who took a stand for Christ. "The fact that I would periodically get phone calls from him was remarkable," said Gregory Thornbury. "I didn't know him well, but that meant the world."[5]

One young voice Colson spent a great deal of time with was worldview apologist John Stonestreet, who cohosted *BreakPoint* with Colson and is presently the program's cohost with Eric Metaxas. Stonestreet recalled that in 2010 Colson told him that he [Colson] was likely in his final years. While Stonestreet was working with Summit Ministries in Colorado, Colson expressed his desire to have the young thinker join his team: "He had me over to his house, and I had lunch with him and Patty. We had a great conversation, and then yes, it was on." Stonestreet remembered Colson's magnetic pull: "You're not going to say no to Chuck Colson. He said he might only have two years left. He had this kind of premonition. It was true."[6]

───────

Colson was nearing the end, but still full of wit and vigor. He evinced a love for gadgetry. A longtime devotee of his little dictation machine, Colson came to love Apple products. Terwilliger, who traveled constantly with Colson, helped his boss learn to use Siri, the "intelligent personal assistant" that helps users navigate the iPhone. Patty was no fan of Chuck's iPad, perhaps because he talked with Siri too much. Colson always enjoyed learning new technologies, even toward the end of his life. "It blew him away when he Skyped for the first time," *BreakPoint* editor David Carlson said. "To him it was a wonder."[7]

Those who worked closely with Colson agreed that he did not put on airs. The boy from hardscrabble Boston never fully changed. Despite the fact he could have enjoyed every luxury available, Colson always flew coach. He enjoyed listening to music on the flight. He loved Henry Gorecki's stirring "3rd Symphony," as he made clear in *How Now Shall We Live?* Colson could glad-hand with the best of them and knew how to engage ultra-wealthy donors and put them at ease. But at the core, he was a man of simple tastes. He loved the salads at Wendy's, Terwilliger noted.[8]

Colson blended high-culture and low-culture instincts. For example, he did not spend much money on clothes, but when he did buy a new suit (or found after a hastily packed exit that he needed strategic garments), he went to Brooks Brothers. Carlson remembered that Colson's constant travel schedule necessitated that his staff "always know where the Brooks Brothers stores were for that reason." When he got home, he sometimes failed to change clothes. Terwilliger reminisced on this point: "I can see him gardening with his black socks up and a tie on."

Life with Colson was never boring. "Traveling with Chuck on the road was always fun," Terwilliger remembered. "Unexpected things always happened. On one trip, we got to a church and Chuck ran to a restroom. A few seconds later, he ran out of the Men's Room. The stalls were occupied." Being a pragmatic type, "he ran into the Women's Room, which was empty. He's in a stall when all of a sudden the door to the room opens up and it's a woman." He later told his staff, laughing uproariously, that "he put his feet up and held them up for five straight minutes so as not to shock her."[9]

Colson enjoyed few things more than a good laugh. He enjoyed the film *National Lampoon's Vacation* (1983), with the scene of "Grandma dying in the car" sending him into gales of laughter, according to Terwilliger. He always read the *New Yorker* and its fabled cartoons. He also carried out his fair share of pranks. He once pulled a doozy on Michael Cromartie. While Cromartie was sleeping one morning, Colson suddenly stormed into his house, leaned over him, and shouted, "Mike, let's go, we're going to be late for the flight!" Cromartie had been told the day before that he wouldn't be traveling with Colson, and he was understandably shocked. He jumped out of bed to fulfill the order, but stopped when he saw his boss convulsed with laughter. Telling the story years later, Cromartie himself couldn't help but laugh.

Despite his tireless work ethic, Colson kept others in mind. He always called "Happy" (his name for Patty) before his airplane took off, telling her he loved her. At other times, he would grab his staffer's hand and pray for him.[10] He did not spend money with impunity; he had a hard time even asking donors for money, though he found a way. But when moved (as he frequently was), he could be tremendously generous. Visiting one Prison Fellowship staffer, he saw immediately that the man did not have what he needed and spontaneously wrote him a large check. When Colson came to the office, he was known as a hugger. Everyone was aware of an imminent "Chuck hug" on days when he was in, Terwilliger said. He knew the names of his staffers and never forgot them.[11]

In the flesh, Colson was what one would expect: dynamic. He lived, as they say, in the moment. But he always had time for those around him, even if his time was carefully apportioned. Evangelical publisher Stan Gundry recalled how Colson interrupted his itinerary on a trip to Grand Rapids, Michigan, for an unscheduled visit with a former prisoner struggling to find his way. The conversation delayed Colson for some time, but he would not break away until he had talked and prayed with his new friend.[12] Once Colson traveled to an Indiana prison with Steven Curtis Chapman, one of the most famous Christian musicians in the world.[13] Colson talked with him for almost half an hour about the dangers of celebrity and fame.

Terwilliger noted that his kindness extended even to those who disagreed strongly with Colson. If the name of an ideological opponent came up, he would interrupt the discussion to pray.

As a boss, Colson created a fun but hard-driving culture. He was loyal to his staff and expected loyalty in return. He also expected hard work. On Fridays at 5:30 p.m., his inner circle knew Colson would likely call in from the road and ask for a report on the week's activities.[14] But the staff loved their leader. Colson drove them hard, but his core team stayed loyal to him, with numerous staffers staying for many years. As a good Marine, Colson led by example. He expected hard work, but he himself worked punishing hours. His staff did not merely perform tasks for his ministry. They knew that he appreciated them, and they took evident joy in working beside him at the plow.

In the closing years of his life, Colson kept working. In 2008 he wrote *The Faith: What Christians Believe, Why They Believe It, and Why It Matters* with Harold Fickett. In a text similar to J. I. Packer's classic *Knowing God*, Colson offered a short but definitive statement of his evangelical theology. The format mirrored that of other Colson works, offering a blend of stories, explanatory passages, and exhortations. It is typically lucid, passionate, and warm.

In a section on God, Colson and Fickett articulated why God's timelessness matters for everyday Christian living: "[A]s Christians we do not need to live oppressed by the ticking clock—the tyranny of the urgent. Life's value doesn't depend upon where we are in time; whether we are young, middle-aged, or old. We see life, all of the time that God created for us, as a gift."[15] Because God has invested all our days with meaning, Colson argued, every person living at every point has value, including both the unborn child and the wizened elder, contra the culture of death. Further, we should make the most of our days, which are a "gift." This blessing "enables us to prepare ourselves for an everlasting relationship with God" and "gives significance to every one of our actions."[16]

When he wrote these words, Colson was nearing the end of an expansive career. He was looking back at his life and seeing all of it in expanded perspective. In his elderly years, he was preparing himself to go to the Lord and to see him face-to-face. One detects an element of personal experience in this prose. Colson had long felt the urgency of the "ticking clock," but he had a sense that it would not tick for a great while longer.

Mortality did not fill Colson with dread. In *The Faith*, he made plain that embracing orthodoxy brought joy. "Is there anything more exciting than to know that you are part of God's great drama that has been played out through history?" he queried his readers. "That you are taking your place alongside the saints who have gone before you?" The faithful Christian, he suggested, is "with Luther at the Diet of Worms, with Augustine when Rome fell, with Aquinas as he wrote his magnificent opus, the *Summa Theologica*."[17] The post-prison Colson had drunk deeply from the well of church history. The zeal he discovered for tracing the hand of God in history never waned.

Colson longed for the next generation of believers to demonstrate the joyful toughness necessary to join the fight in their own day. He reminded the church of the need for it to speak on behalf of the weak: "The Bible itself singles out marginalized groups, the outcasts of society, the beaten-down and trampled upon, the forgotten. The Kingdom has come to deliver sight to the blind, set the prisoners free, feed the hungry, and give hope to the forgotten." Colson's brand of Christianity was grounded in "radical, true liberation."[18] But it was not enough to gaze back at heroes of yesterday. Christians needed to wake up to this call and own it for themselves. "The faith, which once built the greatest civilization in human history, must now engage in the titanic struggle of our times."[19]

Here was Colson's life creed summed up in a few short sentences. His God-given role in the kingdom was to go to the needy, the suffering, and the forgotten, and to minister grace to them. He did not offer heart-warming religion or modifiable piety. Colson proclaimed "radical, true liberation," a term that speaks afresh to his own background. As a former prisoner, disgraced in the public eye, he never lost sight of just how freeing the gospel truly was. He knew what it was to have lost everything, to be at the mercy of routines and regulations that were not of his choosing, and to taste shame and guilt that left only to return.

But more than this, he knew what it was to walk out of a prison a free man, radically and truly liberated, never to return to his cell. This was what he believed Christianity promised the sinner: total transformation. The church existed to preach this saving and renewing gospel. But it would not do so in repose, in quiet days of undisturbed ministry. In 2011, it would need to preach Christ and to act in his name in the midst of nothing less than "titanic struggle."

Chuck Colson saw ahead. Just a few years later, the church would be plunged into a fight on multiple fronts for the preservation of basic freedoms. Seeing this dynamic, Colson took one of the more noteworthy steps of his career when, in 2012, he shared that the need for civil disobedience might arise, should prevailing trends continue. The impetus for this call was the passage of the Obama administration's HHS mandate. The law called for businesses to include coverage of birth control, including some products that could cause abortions, in the health care they provided to employees.

Colson responded by recording a video in which he said that he would disobey his government were this provision enforced: "We have come to the point—I say this very soberly—when if there isn't a dramatic change is circumstances, we as Christians may well be called upon to stand in civil disobedience against the actions of our own government." This was no small undertaking, as Colson knew: "That would break my heart as a former Marine Captain loving my country, but I love my God more . . . I've made up my mind—sober as that decision would have to be—that I will stand for the Lord regardless of what my state tells me."[20]

This charge came at a time when he and many others felt grave concern over the course of American society. But there were trends that gave him great hope too. One of these was the emergence of gifted young Christian thinkers and leaders. One of them was

Eric Metaxas, who worked with Colson at *BreakPoint* as a young man and, years later, was asked by Colson to speak at and emcee the "Breaking the Spiral of Silence" conference in Washington, DC. The friendship between the two men was real, and had only strengthened in recent days. But time was short for Colson, much shorter than anyone around him knew. The night of the conference was in fact the final public event of Chuck Colson's life.

It was the evening of March 30, 2012. The "Breaking the Spiral of Silence" conference was a major event for the Colson Center for Christian Worldview. It brought together Robbie George, Timothy George, Maggie Gallagher, Bishop Harry Jackson, and honored Joni Eareckson Tada. The theme was vintage Colson: "For too long, Christians have been cowed into silence when it comes to the sanctity of human life, traditional marriage, and religious freedom. Join a movement to learn how to stand up, speak out, and break the Spiral of Silence."[21] The conference content encapsulated the burden of Colson's ministry in his final two decades. A consummate performer, even when tired, he thrilled to champion human dignity and religious freedom.

After Metaxas's introduction, Colson took the stage to thunderous applause, with Metaxas, Timothy George, and Colson Center leader John Stonestreet just six feet behind him. But something was amiss. Colson's legs were giving way, and so Metaxas and Stonestreet got him a chair. He began again, but then lapsed into a lengthy silence. He started again, and then went silent once more. Metaxas knew this "was excruciating for him."[22] Event organizers then played a video, but Colson was not watching it from his chair. He was sweating profusely and became sick. By this point, event personnel knew something was terribly amiss. He was taken away in a wheelchair.

A break was held during which Metaxas walked out into the lobby, where he found Colson on a stretcher. "There was nobody standing next to him. I wanted to protect him, and in a half-joking way I said, "Let me know if there's anything you want me to share with the crowd." Ever the gentleman, Colson replied, "Tell them I'm so sorry to have ruined everybody's evening." Metaxas responded: "We'll try hard to forgive you, Chuck." This was the final interaction between the two men. The next day, Alan Terwilliger told Metaxas and others that Colson had a blood clot on his brain, he had suffered a stroke, and he was undergoing an operation. At this point Jim Liske, CEO of Prison Fellowship, and Terwilliger took Metaxas aside. "They asked if I would think about being the voice of *BreakPoint*, which had never occurred to me. I was thunderstruck; I had expected Chuck to do it for another ten years."[23]

Metaxas and Stonestreet teamed up to take over the broadcast, working with *BreakPoint* editor David Carlson. During this time, Terwilliger stayed close to Colson. "I was with him every day during his brain hemorrhage. Halfway between his stupor and being awake, he was talking about unity of the body of the Christ. It didn't make total sense, but it was like this was seared on his brain and that was the message God was giving him."[24] Colson had been talking about the church's unity in his final spate of addresses. It was this theme that played in his mind as he lay dying.

Per his instruction, Colson was not kept alive by unnatural means. With his strong will, he held on to life for three weeks. The family and its friends knew the end was near. Colson had left some basic directions about his funeral. He wanted something simple at his home church, First Baptist of Naples, Florida.

"Chuck wasn't pomp and circumstance," Carlson said.[25] But Terwilliger knew Colson was an evangelical statesman, and that it befit his stature to not only have a service at his church, but another in Washington, DC. Plans were made even as Colson remained alive—though one network twice prematurely reported his passing. Surrounded by his family and close associates, Colson died on April 21, 2012. Though he did not actually die on the podium in Washington, his career and his life effectively ended while Colson was working, devoting himself to the task of cultural engagement, his God-given ministry. The old soldier died, as they say, with his boots on.

MEMORIAL SERVICE

Colson's memorial service was held at the National Cathedral in Washington on Wednesday, May 16, 2012, at 10:00 a.m. The beautiful, awe-inspiring setting was a proper venue for considering a large life lived to the glory of God. Tributes to Colson poured in from all over. US Senator John McCain said simply, "RIP Chuck Colson—a fine man whose life proved that there is such a thing as redemption."

This was a common theme among Colson's eulogists. Writer Michael Gerson, Colson's former research assistant, said that Colson was a "thoroughly converted man," a marvelous summation of the man.[26] "Chuck was possessed," Gerson remembered, "not by some cause, but by someone." Gerson's testimony echoed that of journalist Bob Woodward, who had chronicled the fall of the Nixon administration in painstaking detail: "When Colson went to prison, he experienced, I think, a really genuine conversion and devoted himself to prisoners and prison reform. In a way you can't question [him] because you talk to people in the prison reform movement and Chuck Colson is a god."[27]

Evangelist Billy Graham remembered that "for more than thirty-five years, Chuck Colson, a former prisoner himself, has had a tremendous ministry reaching into prisons and jails with the saving Gospel of Jesus Christ." Graham spoke to his own homegoing: "When I get to Heaven and see Chuck again, I believe I will also see many, many people there whose lives have been transformed because of the message he shared with them." Liske shared that "Chuck was an endlessly selfless man, whose love for and ministry to those in prison made him one of the great modern-day lions of the faith." Richard Land of the Southern Baptist Convention suggested that "if there were an evangelical Mt. Rushmore, Chuck would be on it."[28]

Other tributes came from less well-known circles. Over the years Colson visited Angola prison, the Louisiana State Penitentiary, numerous times, considered one of the toughest correctional facilities in America. Its nickname is "Alcatraz of the South." Colson never shrank from the challenge; he loved going to Angola. Few situations brought out the fearless Colson spirit like the prospect of visiting those who seemed beyond redemption. When Colson's pastor Hayes Wicker visited Angola after Colson's death, he found the inmates in mourning. "We love Chuck Colson," they said to Wicker. "Many of us are saved and in the ministry because of Chuck." Angola inmates had started churches within the prison because of Colson's witness. When they heard of his death, these same inmates made a casket for Colson from wood. They sent it on to Washington in memoriam.[29]

Several stirring addresses were given at the memorial

service. Emily Colson remembered her father in glowing terms, describing his deep love for his grandson Max and some humorous aspects of his personality, including his penchant for time management. Danny Croce, a former prisoner, spoke to the power of the gospel evidenced in Colson's ministry to prisoners. Timothy George movingly captured how Colson's public square work centered in the "ecumenism of the trenches," a bridging of denominational gaps to speak on behalf of the voiceless.

Metaxas believes that the urgency Colson felt to champion fading virtues and Christian positions is waning among believers. "I'm sickened by Christians who think they're too pure to dirty their hands to vote for someone who is not on the same exact page as they are. This stance isn't neutral. If you take it, you're working against God's purposes in our time."[30] The genius of Colson, Metaxas pointed out, was that ministry did not mean someone was perfect but that person was engaged. "Chuck saw that the point of life was not about being pure, but about doing something for the Lord. Marriage and religious freedom are the crucial issues of our day. Of course it would be wonderful to find ourselves in a world in which we would not even have to think about this stuff."

The heroes Metaxas and Colson both wrote about found otherwise, however. They could not choose their battles, but had to fight them for the glory of God and the good of mankind: "Bonhoeffer and Wilberforce were forced into these kind of struggles. If young Christians shrink from politics because they are so pious and politics are so dirty, that breaks God's heart because human hearts are in the balance."

Chuck Colson's life and work demonstrate the truthfulness of this statement. He was able to preach the gospel even as he was able to champion prison reform. He could both witness to the power of conversion and deconstruct an incoherent worldview. Colson saw, furthermore, that there is no tension between loving the gospel and advocating ethical action. The gospel awakens our hearts and opens our eyes to see there is a way of life and of witness that honors God and promises to bless our neighbor.

The Scripture is not intended only for private consumption, and the gospel cannot be bound. One can no more privatize the Word of God than oxygen. God's truth is meant to seep into every area of life. Though cultural transformation will be halting, limited, and only rarely sweeping in its scope, believers are called to be salt and light so that the salt preserves as much of the society as it can and the light reaches as far into the darkness as possible. We are reminded of the early church's witness in ancient Rome. The faithful preaching and sacrificial witness of the early Christians commended the gospel of Christ to the Romans, who converted to Christianity in hordes despite the fact it was an outlawed religion.[31]

We are increasingly in a first-century context, albeit with twenty-first-century trappings. Our faith seems ever more strange to a secularizing culture. In such a time, it is not anger that will sustain us through many fiery trials in our public-square witness, our intervention for the unborn, our caring for the fatherless. It is a big vision of God and his kingdom, one that yields joy and happiness that the world cannot snatch away. This is how, in the end, we dream big dreams and hatch grand plans: we look up to God, the author and finisher of our faith and then, our hearts full, we plunge into our world, confident in him, unafraid of death, knowing that we will live with him as we never have when our earthly sojourn ends.

———

In one season or another, in places all over the world, Christians have often found themselves in just this kind of position: attenuated, uncertain, but sent by God to just this place in just this time. This kind of conviction animated Chuck Colson until he finished the race. Colson's example in his elderly years reminds us of the words of Dylan Thomas: "Do not go gentle into that good night." The Welsh poet's verse speaks to the encroachment of death, but his words capture a biblical posture toward life that Colson exemplified. No matter what he faced, Chuck Colson did not go quietly. He did not fail to put up a fight.

Whether serving as sea monster to his grandson or rebuking the spirit of a secular age, Colson continually sought to push back evil and promote righteousness. He could not be silent; he could not fail to act. He did not work out of a sense of anger or fear. He worked until the end out of a sense of love for his neighbor and commitment to his God. "Faithfulness not success" read the epigram on an old block of wood that sat on his desk. "Do your duty," he continually preached, "and stay at your posts."

As for him, so for us.

EIGHT

ONWARD

The largely unknown story of a tired old man in a small English village captures the spirit of this book.

The philosopher Roger Scruton had a rocky relationship with his father, Jack. Jack was not a man who excelled at communicating with his family. He was emotionally detached and became even more so after his wife died. By Roger's account, his father spent most of his time by himself, alone with his thoughts, disconnected from the broader world.

The family lived in a little town called High Wycombe in England. In the late twentieth century, the local government decided it was time to replace the charming, traditional architecture of High Wycombe with modern architecture. This involved leveling the "organic townscapes that were the homes of real and living communities, and erecting faceless office blocks on their ruins."[1] At first, Jack Scruton heard the news with indifference. What could one do in a world of such change? But then something stirred in the old man. "He looked out from his solitude at what was happening beyond the window of the living room," his son remembered, "and declared uncompromising war on it."

For weeks afterward, Jack went door-to-door in his community. He talked with neighbors he had avoided for decades. He looked people in the eye he had not seen for years. He threw his heart and soul into the campaign to save his town. What woke this man from his slumber? It was not only a concern in architecture or the local community. These things mattered, but there was something deeper. What galvanized this quiet man to action was the possibility of hope.

Hope, however, was not found in this instance in creating a new order. It was located, oddly enough, in preserving all that was good about High Wycombe. Jack Scruton opened his eyes to the plight of his town and saw that progress would not in this case make good on its promises. It would destroy a place that, though imperfect, had gifted him and many others with a quiet, pleasant life. Decisions by bureaucrats were going to forever remake the character of his hometown, replacing the cherished and personal with the generic and faceless.

This was more than a new building plan, a revised city layout. This was a threat to liberty, to beauty, and to the hope of the future. Something of an ancient way of life still lived in High Wycombe. It had not died. It was a gift to those who would come after, for it would fit them into a noble and unique corner of civilization, one that had not been demolished by modern forces and rendered faceless, nameless, by the government. This threat was worth the risk of action. It summoned Jack Scruton to involvement, and it led to the preservation of a small English town that most people will never hear of.

This story fits elegantly with the vision unfolded in this book. Like Jack Scruton, but on a much larger scale, Chuck Colson was a man whose conscience would not allow him to tolerate injustice. Where truth, goodness, and beauty were opposed, he could not sit still. He had to stand up, put boots on the ground, and do all he could to preserve the virtuous and promote the righteous. Though he did not use the label, he was a true progressive, for he cared about the future enough to preserve the good. Colson acted and spoke and agitated in great and small ways on behalf of the permanent things (life, hope, liberty, and virtue) and the institutions (family, church, and conscionable state) that stewarded them.

Colson was a very gifted man. He was bold. He was stalwart. He was unusually courageous and abnormally prophetic. But he was a person just like you and me. He had access to power in a way that most of us do not, but the core of his life was activism in the name of Jesus Christ. Though his ministry merited many headlines, it was in reality a localized work. On many days, Chuck Colson visited prisoners. He preached to small groups. He heard the stories of people whose lives were considered ruined, and he told these people of hope in Jesus Christ and his gospel. He talked behind the scenes to national and global leaders, urging them to stand for what was good and true in the world. He solicited donations for his organization, answered e-mails, dictated memos, and did the hard, small, quiet work that every person must do in his or her vocation.

Chuck Colson was a strong leader, but he was not a super-Christian. He was an imperfect man. Summing up his personality, Eric Metaxas said, "Chuck was Donald Rumsfeld as a Christian." Even in his older years, "he was still quite tough— but always affable."[2] He had his flaws. He worked too hard, made his schedule too full, and sometimes spoke too strongly. But Colson never stopped working to advance truth and goodness.

He wanted to *instantiate* these ideals in culture, to plant them in the ground, so that they would take root, grow up, and lend health to public life. This was not an instinct of his own making.

When God prizes something as universally good, he seems to have a desire to localize it. He creates a people for himself; he sends his Son to be the embodiment of holiness; he expresses his will in a book. The drive to instantiate, to plant, and to concretize what is virtuous is divine.

This kind of enterprise is never private. It is always public. Such work seeks the good of others, a commitment that necessitates breaking out of the solace of our own quiet lives and engaging our world with the gospel. This is crucial for us to understand as we close this book. Young Christians of the millennial generation and those to come are being told they need to keep their beliefs to themselves. We're forcing our morality on other people, it is said, and that is wrong. We are told the very nature of moral judgments is out-of-bounds.

But our friends who say this fail to comprehend the irony of their words. They themselves make moral judgments. No one can help doing so. Even as our culture increasingly faults believers for speaking up on behalf of truth and goodness, it does the same. It is not morality that is the problem. Our culture is divided over which morality is best, and over which narrative is ideal.

What is really at stake today is not just morality. It is the good life. In all our public-square witness we are offering the world a picture of life as it is meant to be. We cannot perfectly capture God's intention for our lives. But our moral vision, our gospel activism, and our cultural engagement do not exist for their own sake. They are parts of a whole—components of a bigger vision. We believe that God wants humanity to flourish. He has created

a life filled with happiness and health that he describes and pre-
scribes in Scripture. In short, the good life given us by God is a
holy life. It has private and public dimensions. It is an existence
committed to God in every facet of our beings. Life of this kind
yields the joy for which we were made.

Christians are not *ultimately* trying to win arguments. We
want to make the best arguments we can, and we hope they prove
persuasive to our society. But we have a broader call and a bigger purpose than any one debate represents. We are promoting
the good life, a life fueled by a theocentric moral imagination.
We do not wish to make life smaller, living out our piety in
self-contained misery, but to make it bigger, living out the joy
of the God-centered life in the noise and activity of our God-
created world. We do not want to drain the vigor out of life, but
to re-enchant it.

The public-square witness of the Christian church points us
beyond what we can see. It suggests there is a world beyond our
own, a true world, which beckons to us. This world is rational
and intelligible, ruled by an intelligence that is in fact divine, but
not rationalistic.[3] It exceeds the bounds of our comprehension
and floods all our circuits. It is the God-made world. This world
is true reality. It is not separate from our own realm, but is present, found everywhere we see truth, beauty, and goodness. We
are citizens of this heavenly kingdom, even as we continue to be
citizens of this earth. We make our pilgrimage to the kingdom
that will last forever through the territory of the kingdom that
will soon crumble.

This dual identity is hard to understand but crucial to
embrace. It points us to the duty of involvement in this sphere
that we have considered from the vantage point of Chuck

Colson's life. We are not only citizens of heaven, which if true would remove any sense of responsibility to this fallen place. We are not only citizens of earth, which if true would remove any need for worship of the living God. We must serve God *here*. Having seen the exultant happiness of the city of God, we must work before night falls to bring it into the city of man.

This framework clarifies our mission even as it necessitates it. We do not have the luxury of creating our own sealed-off cultures without any concern for our neighbor. The church is a corporate witness to the same realities we individually champion. We are able to savor the joy of fellowship in unity, but the church must never be isolated from the world. Christians who buy in to isolationist thinking have lost sight of the biblical imperatives discussed throughout this book.

At the center of the church's witness is the reality of conversion. We need to recover a belief in God and his gospel. We want to see the gospel as saving our souls *and* reorienting our whole existence around God. We are not one body working at many purposes. We are one body working to fulfill the Great Commission by making disciples through the plain and simple preaching of the good news of Jesus Christ.

The church's foremost purpose is the preaching of the Word and its gospel. As pastors declare the whole counsel of Scripture, preaching the Old and New Testaments alike with Jesus at the center, they cannot help but awaken the conscience and shape the ethics of their people. They will not need to preach political homilies to arrest the attention of the flock on cultural and civil matters. They will equip their own local congregations to be a witness wherever they are found.

If we relinquish this work, few will take it up. Too often we think we need not enter into the fray because there are many other people more fitted for the work than we are. This is usually incorrect. Once you engage a momentous issue, as every Christian should, you are startled to find just how few there are beside you. In increasing measure, we will find ourselves nearly alone on the momentous cultural and political issues of the day. The church now finds itself where it so often has been through the ages: pressed on all sides but standing in the gap on behalf of the defenseless. In other words, the odds are right where we want them to be. It is in exactly these kinds of circumstances that our Lord delights to reward a faithful witness.

We do not welcome desperate times, of course. We do know from the biblical stories of Abraham, Joseph, Deborah, Ruth, Hannah, David, Esther, Job, and Daniel that God empowers his people in hardship. Our age calls us to return to the Bible's portraits of these ordinary heroes. These were people just like us who exercised great faith in terrible times. Our own situation looks more and more like those of so many righteous Old Testament Christians. They were not usually the majority. They fought evil both inside and outside the camp. They were scorned by foreign enemies and discouraged even by their loved ones. Yet by God's covenantal grace, they persevered. They did not give in to despair.

In my devotional life I find myself returning again and again to these stories. In many cases, these everyday believers were not called of God to be faithful in private moments, but in profoundly public ones. Deborah roused timid Barak to action in the face of Sisera's devastating attacks. Esther had to contend for the lives of the Jews in the court of Persia, the world superpower at the time. Daniel prayed and testified to his faith before the Babylonian elite. Not all of us will stand before kings, but our faith, too, must be exercised not only in the privacy of our homes but in public, in our workplaces, schools, governments, playgrounds, and everywhere God would have us go.

This advocacy speaks to our broader perspective: we are not culture warriors. We are witnesses. I mean this in the richest, fullest sense. The apostles of Jesus Christ were witnesses. This did not only mean that they had physically seen Christ—as they had—but that they had been transformed by Christ through a personal encounter with him. They could not shut themselves up in their rooms, however. They could not lose themselves in rapturous contemplation of their time with Jesus. They were called and commissioned to go and tell others of this Savior. That was their very identity.

We, too, are witnesses. There is no better term to capture our identity than this. We're not out to intellectually bludgeon our opponents. We're not excited about imperial politics. We're not defenders of a bygone age that our contemporaries have rejected. We are witnesses unto life. This is true in numerous respects in 2015.

We are witnesses as family members. The church relishes the beauty of the natural family, the special creation of an ultra-intelligent designer. It is God who created man and woman. It is God who made them different but complementary. It is God who gave them the institution of marriage, a covenantal relationship ordained to bless the man and woman and to picture the love of God's Son for his people. The church cannot stop promoting the goodness of the family in the public square because the church wants to love its neighbors and lead them to flourishing life.

The family that makes a life together is showing the world

the architecture of love. But we need not be married to experience the sustaining pleasure of God and offer the world a vibrant witness. The single person has a tremendous opportunity to show that our happiness is not bound up with sex. God is enough. We do not need to be a father or mother to serve the Lord. In fact, we have perhaps greater opportunities to live single-mindedly for Christ when we are not married (1 Cor. 7). The church needs to support a marriage culture *and* to support singles as leading valuable lives in God's sight. For many, the commitment to singleness is not easy. It is a daily choice, though, one that looks strangely like taking up our cross and following Jesus all the way to our joyful end.

We are witnesses to the goodness of sex. We recognize that sex is not its own end. It has been given us for a purpose. It is the ultimate personal expression of covenantal love. The union of a husband and wife images the love of a crucified Savior for his bride, the church (Eph. 5:22–33). The church is not squeamish about sex or embarrassed by it. Sex was created for pleasure. But we only truly taste pleasure when we know its purpose and when we honor the design of God's gifts. The body is not given us as a vehicle of self-expression, primarily, but as a means of God-glorification (1 Cor. 10:31). There is little testimony in the Bible that would lead us to remake or substantially alter our bodies. There is abundant evidence that we have been given our bodies to taste God's goodness, and to honor him by wise stewardship.

Our convictions here run counter to our culture. Phase one of our postmodern cultural makeover targeted the mind. We are all tempted to be relativists now—at least until someone questions our views or disagrees with our claims, in which we morph rather quickly into authoritarians. Phase two of this shift is targeting the body. The project to normalize and sanctify same-sex marriage, homosexual orientation, and transgender identity is powered by a postmodern understanding of the body. There is no grand design of our form and frame, no story that our bodies are telling. We are blank slates, and we may do with our bodies whatever we like.

In light of such thinking, the church must speak to the goodness of God's design. Our bodies are a crucial part of our discipleship. Our identity as a man and a woman matters greatly for biblical obedience. We are not nervous about sex, but neither do we buy in to a sexualized culture that grounds our humanity in sexual acts. The church is a witness to the beauty of God's creation, and even as our peers give in to lusts of the flesh and the desire to overhaul themselves, we must help them see that the new sexual ethos will not make good on its promises.

We are witnesses of true freedom. No concept is more discussed today; none is more misunderstood. I have read no more powerful portrait of our modern misunderstanding of personal liberty than in Jonathan Franzen's novel *Freedom*. Though no conservative, Franzen traced the effects of a culture of autonomous freedom on one Minnesota couple, Walter and Patty. Their marriage dissolves as they drift apart, and they travel far from each other in their wanderings. In the book's conclusion, they return to each other, putting away years of bitter selfishness:

> And so he stopped looking at her eyes and started looking into them, returning their look before it was too late, before this connection between life and what came after life was lost, and let her see all the vileness inside him, all the hatreds of two thousand solitary nights, while the two of them were

still in touch with the void in which the sum of everything they'd ever said or done, every pain they'd inflicted, every joy they'd shared, would weigh less than the smallest feather on the wind.[4]

Like this fictional couple, we are tempted today to believe that we will be free and happy when we follow our own selfish hearts. This has tragic consequences for families. So we divorce, break ties, abandon our children. Our journeys are borne aloft by personal freedom, unconstrained and disconnected, but like Icarus, we crash to the ground. We must make clear that hope is found not in looking past our loved ones, but looking into their eyes, to use Franzen's image.

We are witnesses to gospel reconciliation when we cross racial divides as believers. Christians are those who make friends with people who naturally have nothing in common with us. We show the world how the Lord changes us when we forge relationships with people we would never countenance were it not for the image of God and the cross of Christ. We must pursue racial reconciliation, whether our efforts are public or private. We cannot content ourselves with knowing people from the comfort of set-apart difference. It is our calling to make a genuine attempt to enter into their own self-understanding, and to make good on the fact that the church is one body, one "new man," as the apostle Paul said (Eph. 2:15).

We are witnesses to the goodness of government, and also to its limits. We are not anti-government in principle; we know that Jesus saw Caesar as a legitimate authority and that Christians are called wherever possible to be peaceable and productive citizens (Matt. 22:21; 1 Tim. 2:2). But we do not ask the state to serve spiritual ends, and we stand against the tide that would render it an omnipresent guide. Many Christians recognize the virtue not only of federal government, but also of state and local government. Civic life is a part of the good life. We have agency, duties, and opportunities to work alongside our neighbor to promote what is good and oppose what is wrong.

We are witnesses to the importance of neighbor-love, of community, as it is sometimes called. We want to be rooted people, to plant ourselves somewhere to instantiate the goodness of God and enjoy the pleasures of what Paul called "a peaceful and quiet life, godly and dignified in every way" (1 Tim. 2:2). This kind of mind-set, however, requires that we reenvision our lives. "People are living as if they think they are in a movie," Wendell Berry once wrote.[5] We are not movie stars. We are something far better: neighbors, friends, agents of grace. We want not only to know the people in our neighborhoods, but to love them. As Rod Dreher has said: "Accept the limitations of a place, in humility, and the joys that can also be found there may open themselves."[6]

Our involvement in local churches is a key part of our localized Christianity. Long before urban reclamation became popular and farm-to-table went global—a minor irony, this— ordinary believers practiced a richly local existence. The church of Jesus Christ is universal, one body over all the times and places of the earth. But it is always called to be local. God loves to particularize his kingdom. We will glorify him and strengthen our own witness and walk as Christians by joining a local church, serving it, and partnering with fellow members to love our neighbors in word and deed.[7]

We are witnesses to the goodness of work. We recall the term the Protestant Reformers used to sum up a God-centered view of work: *vocatio,* "vocation." The nomenclature is important. You *do* a job; you *inhabit* and are *called* to a vocation. Matthew Crawford has said that our daily labor in our vocation speaks to "the permanent, local viability of what is best in human beings." Against a mechanized order that reduces us all to automatons, Crawford championed "seeking out the cracks where individual agency and the love of knowledge can be realized today, in one's own life."[8] From a theistic angle, we see our work as a little picture of God's own activity. Our tasks, great and small, have value.

Because we work unto God, *coram deo,* all our virtuous work is important. Calling voters matters; folding tiny baby clothes matters; teaching students matters; defending civilizations against terror matters; creating wealth matters. It is easy to underplay the goodness of the free market, but we should not submit ourselves easily to stereotypes. A 2011 study from Yale University and the Brookings Institute showed, for example, that the percentage of the world's population living below the extreme poverty line has been reduced from 52 percent in 1981 to 15 percent in 2011. According to the study, three major factors account for this shift: "the rise of globalization, the spread of capitalism and the improving quality of economic governance."[9]

Many Christians tune out when they hear talk about either governmental or economic matters. Government, we conjecture, can't possibly relate to spiritual concerns, and economics matters only to math nerds. The opposite is true. The state relates to our spiritual lives; its size and scope of activity directly relate to the conditions of our faith. So, too, with economics. If we have no ability to create wealth, we stay impoverished, living in conditions that pose harm for our spiritual well-being. Of course, Christian faith can thrive in the worst of settings, whether in totalitarian regimes or extreme poverty. But we do not wish to create such conditions. We recognize the goodness of God's provision, seeing in the act of creation itself a signal that ours is not a limited world. There is no check on well-being. Our lives always bear the possibility of improvement, and God's resources are not growing scarce.

We are witnesses unto life, particularly the life of the unborn child. Christians know that God loves even the least of our world. He is the one who has created life. He loves it. Satan loves death; death is his work, his transcultural project, and abortion driven by personal preference is one of his most devious initiatives. Young evangelicals do not have the choice of "opting out" from pro-life ministry. Every believer has the duty, the delightful duty, of promoting and creating a culture of life.

Our mission is not to recover a former vision of America but to faithfully represent our king, Jesus Christ, in a lost realm, the city of man. We are *contra mundum*—against the world, as Colson's *Christianity Today* column was called. But we are also *pro mundum*—for the world. We do not *hate* our neighbors in opposing evil, for example. We oppose evil, by contrast, in order to *love* our neighbors. *Contra mundum pro mundo.* We are against the world for the world, as Colson's friend Richard John Neuhaus used to say.[10]

Our identity as witnesses speaks to our nature as the true culture, as Stanley Hauerwas has said. The church is the people of God. We have not made ourselves into acceptable servants of Christ. God in his mercy has redeemed us and given us the name and nature that transcends the world. All around us is untruth and falsehood. "[T]he light has come into the world," Jesus said, "and people loved the darkness rather than the light because their works were evil. For everyone who does wicked things hates the light and does not come to the light, lest his works should be exposed" (John 3:19–20). In its sinful, lost state, the human heart hates Christ, strong as those words sound. Outside of Jesus, we belong to this anticulture.

The church is the true culture that brings the light into all the world. To do so, we must often be a counterculture. We will often be opposed, hated, and mocked. We will be persecuted in small and great ways. Jihadist Islam has not diminished as a global threat to peace and stability, after all. Atheism and the amoral code it yields is a serious worldview competitor to Christianity. A sexualized culture promises tolerance but sharply polices dissidents. In the face of such forces, we might instinctively shrink back. We might wonder if we are doing it all wrong, if there is a way that we can take the sting out of Christianity such that people see our good intentions.

This is a tempting illusion. Jesus spoke directly to it: "If the world hates you, know that it has hated me before it hated you" (John 15:18). It is precisely because we belong to Christ that we are hated. Young evangelicals must reckon with these words. They sound surprisingly tough to our ears. Perhaps we hear them, but still desire some way—any way—to distance ourselves from needless antipathy. We look up at the doorposts of our homes, the frame that bears a bloody stain. We might feel within ourselves a desire to scrub that crimson mark. We might grow tired of standing out and standing apart. We might wish to affirm what the culture affirms and thus lose our problematic distinctiveness. But we should note the consequences of this desire to remove the scandal of the faith. Once you have whitewashed your houses' doorposts of their bloody stain, you find that your neighbors stop looking at you funny, it's true. But now your house looks just like every other abode in Egypt.

The stakes are high. We can gain the culture, but lose the gospel. In treacherous times like these, we need to be shrewd as serpents and gentle as doves (Matt. 10:16). We should be winsome, kind, and engaging. But we cannot surrender our convictions. There will be no peace treaty with the spiritual forces that wish to silence and overcome us. We do not struggle with flesh and blood, but principalities and powers that despise us to the full. "If you were of the world, the world would love you as its own," Jesus said, "but because you are not of the world, but I chose you out of the world, therefore the world hates you" (John 15:19).

There is no public-relations campaign that can take away the perceived foolishness of Christianity. The gospel is an offense, a stumbling block (1 Cor. 1:22–23). It is not the church, with all its imperfections, that has created these conditions. It is the hatred of God that originated with the fall of Satan and that blazes in every human heart. We will be tempted to play down our convictions, to posture ourselves as beyond disagreement, to relentlessly seek a "third way" in every cultural struggle that enables us to be seen in a positive light. However well intentioned these instincts, they cannot ultimately deliver. The church must not hide its light. It is not our coolness or cultural approval that will win people to the faith. It is our promotion of the truth of God.

If we are to be the true culture, advocating for truth, beauty, and goodness, we must often be a counterculture. We must square with this identity. Not only this: we must see it as a divine calling, as a blessing, as a gift. *Contra mundum pro mundo.* We oppose evil wherever it is found in order that we might love our neighbors and lead them unto God. In this work, we are witnesses. In the final analysis, we have entered the public square out of love—love for God and his Word, and love for our neighbor.

Young evangelicals need these words, for we will only continue to watch as our culture drifts from any Judeo-Christian mooring. Seeing this will sadden us. We should love our country. But this trajectory will not dishearten us. We will not give up. We will not give up our convictions. We will not compromise the truth. We may pay a price for taking this stand; we may lose jobs, our friends, even sever ties with our families. But do not be mistaken; there will be no truce with a secular culture. There will be no surrender of our convictions. The millennials, with all the true church of God, will hold the line, and give the good confession.

We do so with history's conclusion on our minds. Whatever may come, we know we are citizens of a greater kingdom. We are crossing the Jordan to a better land. We are part of a bigger story, a story driven by the truth of Jesus Christ, Savior and Lord over all. This story is beyond us, bigger than us, but also gives us all vital roles to play. It is a story God has authored and that God is bringing to rightful conclusion.

This story is a serious one. It tells of salvation and judgment. But it has a place, if you look deep enough, for irony, perhaps even divine irony. This was certainly true in Chuck Colson's life. Perhaps no event more speaks to the strange providence of his life than his 2008 reception of the Presidential Citizens Medal. In one of the final acts of his two-term presidency, George W. Bush summoned Colson back to the White House to recognize him as a leading contributor to the good of his country. The official citation made clear the indissoluble connection between Colson's faith and his work:

For more than three decades, Chuck Colson has dedicated his life to sharing the message of God's boundless love and mercy with prisoners, former prisoners, and their families. Through his strong faith and leadership, he has helped courageous men and women from around the world make successful transitions back into society. The United States honors Chuck Colson for his good heart and his compassionate efforts to renew a spirit of purpose in the lives of countless individuals.[11]

Colson was deeply moved by the honor. "Whatever good I may have done is because God saw fit to reach into the depths of Watergate and convert a broken sinner," he remarked at the ceremony. "Everything that has been accomplished these past 35 years has been by God's grace and sovereign design."

On this happy day, Patty Colson was by Chuck's side, as she had been for decades. She was understandably proud of her husband, and at this late date in their shared work, thankful for all he had accomplished.[12] Without Patty's support and without the support of Emily, Christian, and Wendell, Colson's efforts would not have gone nearly as far as they did. The Colsons celebrated the medal together.

This was a poignant moment for Colson. He was back in the White House. Here he had felt the intoxicating rush of power and truly global influence. Here he had reached his highest highs. But it was also here that things fell apart for him. As he took in the moment, Colson must have felt gratitude to God for rescuing him from his path of self-destruction. The Lord was kind to Chuck Colson.

For the rest of his life, Colson wore the pin from the medal in his navy blazer.[13] After so much disappointment and trial, he had returned to his old haunts. He was not condemned there but honored. Perhaps, as he savored this development, Colson reflected on a seemingly minor detail, one lost to history: the president who had created the Presidential Citizens Medal was none other than Richard Milhous Nixon.

This ironic twist, as with all the rich and winding life of Chuck Colson, reminds us of the power of God's providence. Young evangelicals may feel that the days are evil and the odds are against us. But God is good. He has not left us without his Word, his Spirit, and his gospel. He does all things well, and he always brings the twists and turns of our lives to their proper conclusion. We cannot leave the public square. Like a certain redeemed prisoner, he has china for us to break.

Treasuring this truth, and acting upon it as a witness, is not something new to our generation, to the millennials. It is as old as the earth. It is the Christian way. For a brief time on this earth, it was—and can be again—the Colson way.

NOTES

INTRODUCTION

1. Eric Metaxas, *Seven Men: And the Secret of Their Greatness* (Nashville: Thomas Nelson, 2013).

CHAPTER 1: ASCENT

1. Chuck Colson, *Born Again* (Peabody, MA: Hendrickson, 2008 [1976]), 28–29.
2. BB&N, http://www.bbns.org/page.cfm?p=645&teamID=115 &display=Overview.
3. Jonathan Aitken, *Charles W. Colson: A Life Redeemed* (Colorado Springs: WaterBrook, 2005), 25–26.
4. Colson, *Born Again*, 12.
5. Aitken, *Colson,* 20.
6. See Morton Keller and Phyllis Keller, *Making Harvard Modern: The Rise of America's University* (Oxford: Oxford University Press, 2007).
7. James Bryant Conant, "Education for a Classless Society: Charter Day Address delivered at the University of California on March 28, 1940," *The Atlantic*, accessible at http://www.theatlantic.com /magazine/archive/1940/05/education-for-a-classless-society/305 254/?single_page=true.
8. Colson, *Born Again*, 15.
9. Brown University, http://www.brown.edu/about/history.

10. "History of the Brunonian Chapter," http://students.brown.edu /Alpha_Delta_Phi/history/brunonian.php.

11. Colson, *Born Again*, 22.

12. Chuck Colson, "Can the Ivy League Teach Ethics?," address at Brown University, May 24, 2003, accessible at http://www.colson center.org/search-library/search?view=searchdetail&id=6969.

13. See Owen Strachan, *Awakening the Evangelical Mind* (Grand Rapids: Zondervan, 2015); Joel Carpenter, *Revive Us Again: The Reawakening of American Fundamentalism* (New York: Oxford University Press, 1997); George Marsden, *The Soul of the American University: From Protestant Establishment to Established Unbelief* (Oxford: Oxford University Press, 1994).

14. Ibid.

15. Colson, *Born Again*, 16.

16. Aitken, *Colson*, 41.

17. Carl Marchi, *Always Faithful: A Marine's Tale* (Bloomington, IN: AuthorHouse, 2007), 54.

18. Chuck Colson, "Can the Ivy League Teach Ethics?"

19. Colson, *Born Again*, 18–21; see also Aitken, *Colson*, 55–65.

20. Aitken, *Colson*, 65–67.

21. Ibid., 66.

22. Colson, *Born Again*, 19–20.

23. *Boston Globe*, "Charles H. Morin: Obituary," accessible at http://www.legacy.com/obituaries/bostonglobe/obituary.aspx ?n=charles-h-morin&pid=93146740#sthash.6kBEiK4H.dpuf.

24. Aitken, *Colson*, 112–14.

25. Ibid., 117.

CHAPTER 2: CONVERSION

1. Richard Nixon, *The Memoirs of Richard Nixon* (New York: Grosset & Dunlap, 1978), 496.

2. Aitken, *Colson*, 128–32.

3. Ibid., 132.

4. Colson, *Born Again*, 61.

5. Ibid., 62–64.

6. Ibid., 72.

7. Ibid., 73.

8. Ibid., 76.

9. For fuller details from Colson's life in this period, see Aitken, *Colson*, 153–91.

10. Colson, *Born Again*, 108–11.

11. See Aitken, *Colson*, 150–53.

12. Ibid., 152–53.

13. For the definitive journalistic account of Watergate, see Carl Bernstein and Bob Woodward, *All the President's Men* (New York: Simon & Schuster, 1974). See also Bob Woodward and Carl Bernstein, *The Final Days* (New York: Simon & Schuster, 1976).

14. Colson, *Born Again*, 124–25.

15. Raytheon Company, *The First 60 Years*, http://books.google .com/books?id=k01hX_bCa10C&pg=PA6&lpg=PA6&dq=tom +phillips+raytheon&source=bl&ots=41h4p4yeEg&sig=XWfs 9w1OLwaLop91oevFaNUdEgw&hl=en&sa=X&ei=vuHDU6T HFcGPyAT5x4LQBg&ved=0CHsQ6AEwDg#v=onepage&q =tom%20phillips%20raytheon&f=false.

16. Colson, *Born Again*, 126–27.

17. Ibid., 129.

18. C. S. Lewis, *Mere Christianity* (Grand Rapids: Zondervan, 1952), 124.

19. Colson, "Thirty-Five Years in the Light," August 12, 2008, http:// descant.wordpress.com/2008/08/25/chuck-colson-reflects-on-his -conversion/.

20. Ibid.

21. Gordon College, "Life, Leadership and Legacy: A Tribute to Tom Phillips," http://www.gordon.edu/article.cfm?iArticleID =798&iReferrerPageID=1676&iPrevCatID=134&bLive=1.

22. Colson, *Born Again*, 139–45.

23. Ibid., 164–73.

24. Aitken, *Colson*, 228–29.

25. Ibid., 230–32.

26. http://law.justia.com/cases/district-of-columbia/court-of-appeals
/1979/24–74–3.html.

CHAPTER 3: PRISON

1. Chuck Colson, "Christmas in Jail," *BreakPoint*, December 25, 2012, http://www.breakpoint.org/bpcommentaries/entry/13 /21086.
2. Ibid.
3. Colson, *Born Again*, 307.
4. Colson, *Life Sentence* (London: Hodder and Stoughton, 1979), 99.
5. Ibid., 98–99.
6. Ibid., 328.
7. Adam Edelman, "Jesse Jackson Jr. Moved to Another Prison After Skirmish with Guards, Solitary Stint: Report," *New York Daily News*, April 7, 2014, http://www.nydailynews.com/news /politics/jesse-jackson-jr-moved-prison-skirmish-guards-solitary -confinement-stint-report-article-1.1748290.
8. Ibid.
9. Greg Garrison, "Prison Fellowship Founder Chuck Colson Visits Alabama Prisons on Easter Weekend," April 23, 2011, http://blog.al.com/spotnews/2011/04/prison_fellowship _founder_chuc.html.
10. Colson, *Born Again*, 403.
11. Ibid., 406–9.
12. Colson, *Life Sentence*, 22.
13. Ibid., 24.
14. Ibid., 71.
15. Baker Publishing Group, http://bakerpublishinggroup.com /chosen/about-chosen.
16. Colson, *Born Again*, xiv.
17. Colson, *Life Sentence*, 47.
18. Ibid., 61.
19. Harold Hughes, *The Man from Ore Ida: A Senator's Personal Story* (Waco, TX: Word, 1979), 73.

20. http://themoderatevoice.com/181727/for-iowa-senator-hughes
    -a-field-of-dreams-story/.

21. Hughes, *The Man from Ore Ida*, 102–3.

22. Ibid., 108.

23. Ibid., 323.

24. Ibid.

25. Colson, *Life Sentence*, 66.

26. Ibid., 67.

27. Ibid., 146–47.

28. Aitken, *Colson*, 335–36.

29. Ibid., 335.

30. Ibid., 336.

CHAPTER 4: ROOTS

1. Aitken, *Colson*, 396.

2. Colson, *Life Sentence*, 152.

3. Ibid., 153.

4. Ibid.

5. Ibid.

6. Aitken, *Colson*, 299.

7. Ibid.

8. Interview with Alan Terwilliger, June 20, 2014.

9. Aitken, *Colson*, 317.

10. See Joanne Hemenway, *Forgot Them Not: A Holistic Guide to Prison Ministry* (New York: Wipf & Stock, 2010).

11. Aitken, *Colson*, 324–25.

12. The official website is http://speakfortheunborn.com.

13. To read more of this experience, see my *Gospel Coalition* essay, "Dodging Haymakers Outside the Abortion Clinic," found at http://www.thegospelcoalition.org/article/dodging-haymakers -outside-the-abortion-clinic.

14. Marvin Olasky, "Experiences Have Consequences," *World*, May 9, 2009, http://www.worldmag.com/2009/05/experiences _have_consequences/page2.

15. Interview with Michael Cromartie, June 18, 2014, Washington, DC.

16. Ibid.

17. Ibid.

18. See James D. Bratt, *Abraham Kuyper: Modern Calvinist, Christian Democrat* (Grand Rapids: Eerdmans, 2013).

19. See Eric Metaxas, *Amazing Grace: William Wilberforce and the Heroic Campaign to End Slavery* (New York: HarperCollins, 2009), 69–80.

20. Colson, *Loving God*, 166.

21. For a brief introduction to Venn, see Owen Strachan, "The Wilberforce Test," 9Marks eJournal (November 2014), accessible at http://www.google.com/url?sa=t&rct=j&q=9marks %20wilberforce%20test&source=web&cd=1&cad=rja&uact=8& ved=0CCAQFjAA&url=http%3A%2F%2F9marks.org%2 Farticle%2Fthe-wilberforce-test-preaching-and-the-public -square%2F&ei=gdmqVPi5EsmNyASqm4HQDA&usg=AFQjC NGFH0vYlkMCKlMP6WekKft3UdrW7A&sig2=o0J8ji2K6n MI9A1HMmkFfQ&bvm=bv.82001339,d.aWw.

22. See Kevin Vanhoozer and Owen Strachan, *The Pastor as Public Theologian: Recovering a Lost Vision* (Grand Rapids: Baker, 2015).

23. Burk Parsons, "R. C. Sproul: A Man Called by God," Ligonier Ministries, http://www.ligonier.org/learn/articles/r-c-sproul -man-called-god/.

24. Colson, *Loving God*, 15.

25. Ibid.

26. I first heard this from TEDS historian John Woodbridge while I was a doctoral student at the divinity school on Chicago's North Shore (2008–11).

27. See Gregory Alan Thornbury, *Recovering Classic Evangelicalism: Applying the Wisdom and Vision of Carl F. H. Henry* (Carol Stream, IL: Crossway, 2013); Matthew J. Hall and Owen Strachan, *Essential Evangelicalism: The Enduring Influence of Carl F. H. Henry* (Carol Stream, IL: Crossway, 2015).

28. Interview with Matt Schmucker, June 18, 2014, Washington, DC.

29. Chuck Colson, "Rest for a Warrior: Remembering Carl Henry," Townhall.com, Dec. 4, 2003, http://townhall.com/columnists /chuckcolson/2003/12/12/rest_for_a_warrior_remembering _carl_henry.

30. Ibid.

31. Paul Vitello, "Edith Schaeffer, Definer of Christian Family Values, Dies at 98," *New York Times*, April 6, 2013, http://www .nytimes.com/2013/04/07/world/europe/edith-schaeffer-98-dies -defined-christian-values.html?_r=0.

32. Barry Hankins, *Francis Schaeffer and the Shaping of Evangelical America* (Grand Rapids: Eerdmans, 2008), 109; see also Colin Duriez, *Francis Schaeffer: An Authentic Life* (Carol Stream, IL: Crossway, 2008).

33. Colson, *Loving God*, 245.

CHAPTER 5: EXPANSION

1. Jodi Werhanowicz, *Rogue Angel: The Spiritual Journey of One of the FBI's Ten Most Wanted* (Phoenix: Ezekiel, 2005), 8–16.

2. Ibid., 72.

3. "Mary Kay's Testimony," Encourager Ministries, http://www .encouragerministries.com/showandtell.asp?id=1900.

4. Werhanowicz, *Rogue Angel*, 128.

5. Encourager Ministries, http://www.encouragerministries.com /showandtell.asp?id=1900.

6. Ibid.

7. Janet Chismar, "An Interview with Angel Tree Founder, Mary Kay Beard," Crosswalk.com, Dec. 13, 2002, http://www.crosswalk .com/faith/spiritual-life/an-interview-with-angel-tree-founder- mary-kay-beard-1176428.html?ps=0.

8. Ibid.

9. Michael Gerson, "Charles Colson Found Freedom in Prison," *Washington Post*, April 22, 2012, http://www.washingtonpost .com/opinions/finding-freedom-in-prison/2012/04/22/gIQAN abcaT_story.html.

10. See http://www.prisonfellowship.org/story/angel-tree-celebrates
-30-years/ and http://www.crosswalk.com/faith/spiritual-life/an
-interview-with-angel-tree-founder-mary-kay-beard-1176428
.html?ps=0.

11. Ibid.

12. Ibid.

13. Janet Chismar, "An Interview with Angel Tree Founder, Mary
Kay Beard," *Crosswalk*, December 12, 2002, accessible at http
://www.crosswalk.com/faith/spiritual-life/an-interview-with
-angel-tree-founder-mary-kay-beard-1176428.html?ps=0.

14. Werhanowicz, *Rogue Angel*, 215–16.

15. Aitken, *Colson*, 339.

16. "Angel Tree Celebrates 30 Years," Prison Fellowship, http://www
.prisonfellowship.org/story/angel-tree-celebrates-30-years/.

17. Chuck Colson, "Christmas Miracles," *BreakPoint*, December 11,
2011, accessible at http://www.breakpoint.org/bpcommentaries
/entry/13/18016?tmpl=component&print=1.

18. See Steve Ercolani, "Baseball League Creates 'Islands' Of
Refuge For Camden Kids," NPR, July 16, 2013, accessible at
http://www.npr.org/2013/07/16/199027063/baseball-league
-creates-islands-of-refuge-for-camden-kids.

19. See John Piper and Wayne Grudem, *Recovering Biblical
Manhood & Womanhood: A Response to Evangelical Feminism*
(Carol Stream, IL: Crossway, 1992); Jonathan Parnell and
Owen Strachan, *Designed for Joy: How the Gospel Shapes
Manhood and Womanhood, Identity and Practice* (Carol
Stream, IL: Crossway, 2015).

20. Aitken, *Colson*, 339.

21. Chuck Colson, "Foreword," in Emily Colson, *Dancing with Max*
(Grand Rapids, MI: Zondervan, 2010), 13.

22. Ibid.

23. Colson, *Dancing with Max*, 15.

24. http://www.newhopecm.org/bio.htm.

25. See http://ruinedfortheordinary.com/understanding-gods

-mercy-and-forgiveness; also Chuck Colson and Nancy Pearcey, *How Now Shall We Live?* (Carol Stream, IL: Tyndale, 1999), 284.

26. Colson and Pearcey, *How Now Shall We Live?*, 288.

27. Ibid., 293.

28. See http://ruinedfortheordinary.com/understanding-gods-mercy -and-forgiveness.

29. Interview with Gregory Thornbury, June 27, 2014, Louisville, Kentucky.

CHAPTER 6: WITNESS

1. Chuck Colson, *Chuck Colson Speaks* (Uhrichsville, OH: Promise, 2000), 171.

2. http://www.saabnet.com/tsn/models/1996/5451.html.

3. "Find Your Own Road Saab Advertising Campaign," Sept. 19, 2007, Saab History, http://www.saabhistory.com/2007/09/19 /find-your-own-road-saab-advertising-campaign.

4. Chuck Colson, "Find Your Own Road: Saab and the Age of Aquarius," *BreakPoint*, July 30, 1997, accessible at http://www .breakpoint.org/commentaries/4698-find-your-own-road.

5. Colson, *Chuck Colson Speaks*, 171. Years later, Manby clearly still did not particularly like the "Find Your Own Road" campaign: "That was in place before I was onboard, and it was successful. However, the head of worldwide advertising in Sweden wanted one consistent campaign and positioning worldwide. While I was not necessarily against the 'find your own road' campaign, I really agreed that a fairly consistent worldwide image was the right way to go."

6. Interview with Hugh Hewitt, November 4, 2014, Louisville, Kentucky. According to Hewitt, Colson did clearly belong to one under-represented group: those who wore dark-framed glasses. "Chuck also popularized the glasses I'm wearing. He had those ridiculous glasses that now everybody wears. I'm not trying to be hip, but now they are. Long before they became a fashion tendency, Chuck wore them." Colson was not a

member of the Religious Right, but he was apparently a hipster without knowing it.

7. Correspondence with Andrew Walker, November 2, 2014.

8. Chuck Colson, *Kingdoms in Conflict* (Grand Rapids, MI: Zondervan, 1987), 229–30.

9. Ibid., 118–21.

10. Ibid., 121.

11. Chuck Colson and Ellen Santilli Vaughn, *The Body: Being Light in Darkness* (Nashville: Thomas Nelson, 1994), 66.

12. Ibid., 71.

13. Hayes Wicker, "FIRST-PERSON: Remembering Chuck Colson, the church member," April 25, 2012, accessible at http://www .bpnews.net/37688/firstperson-remembering-chuck-colson -the-church-member.

14. Interview with Hayes Wicker, January 7, 2015, by phone.

15. Interview with John Michael LaRue, July 13, 2014, Louisville, Kentucky.

16. Interview with Wicker.

17. Randy Boyagoda, *Richard John Neuhaus: A Life in the Public Square* (Colorado Springs: Image, 2015).

18. See Randy Boyagoda, *Richard John Neuhaus: A Life in the Public Square* (Colorado Springs: Image, 2015).

19. See "'Nones' on the Rise," *Pew Report*, October 9, 2012, accessible at http://www.pewforum.org/2012/10/09/nones-on-the-rise.

20. Remarks made on a panel at the Ethics and Religious Liberty Commission National Conference, October 27, 2014. See also Sean McDowell and John Stonestreet, *Same-Sex Marriage: A Thoughtful Approach to God's Design for Marriage* (Grand Rapids, MI: Baker Books, 2014); Denny Burk and Heath Lambert, *Transforming Homosexuality: How to Live Faithfully with Same-Sex Attraction* (Phillipsburg, NJ: P&R, 2015); Sam Allberry, *Is God Anti-Gay?* (Surrey, UK: The Good Book Company, 2013); Rosaria Butterfield, *Secret Thoughts of an Unlikely Convert* (Pittsburgh: Crown and Covenant, 2012).

21. See Owen Strachan, "College Sex Classes Are Destroying Sex," *The Federalist*, October 29, 2014, accessible at http://thefederalist.com/2014/10/29/college-sex-classes-are-destroying-sex.

22. Tom Wolfe, *Hooking Up* (New York: Picador, 2001), 9.

23. For more on the sinfulness of homosexual desire and practice, see Robert A. J. Gagnon, *The Bible and Homosexual Practice: Texts and Hermeneutics* (Nashville: Abingdon, 2001); R. Albert Mohler, Jr., ed., *God and the Gay Christian? A Response to Matthew Vines* (Louisville: SBTS Press, 2014).

24. See Courtney Reissig, *The Accidental Feminist: Restoring Our Delight in God's Good Design* (Carol Stream, IL: Crossway, 2015); Andreas and Margaret Kostenberger, *God's Design for Man and Woman: A Biblical-Theological Survey* (Carol Stream, IL: Crossway, 2014).

25. See the prescient study of American culture by George Marsden, *The Twilight of the American Enlightenment: The 1950s and the Crisis of Liberal Belief* (New York: Basic, 2014).

26. See the "Author Bio" on this page: http://www.christianbook.com/born-again-ebook-charles-colson/9781585589418/pd/12602EB.

27. http://centurionsprogram.org/wp-content/uploads/2014/02/Centurions_Brochure_Web.pdf.

28. Interview with R. Albert Mohler, Jr., December 4, 2014, Louisville, Kentucky.

29. Broward Liston, "Interview: Missionary Work in Iraq," *TIME*, April 15, 2003, accessible at http://content.time.com/time/world/article/0,8599,443800,00.html.

30. Interview with Erick Erickson, January 8, 2015, by phone.

31. Interview with Matthew Schmitz, June 20, 2014, New York City.

32. Visit http://studycentersonline.org/ for more information.

33. http://www.templetonprize.org/previouswinner.html.

34. Colson, *Chuck Colson Speaks*, 15.

35. Ibid., 19.

36. Ibid., 22.

37. See Jonathan Hill, *What Has Christianity Ever Done for Us?: How it Shaped the Modern World* (Downers Grove, IL: InterVarsity, 2005); Alvin J. Schmidt, *How Christianity Changed the World* (Grand Rapids: Zondervan, 2004).

38. Interview with Hugh Hewitt, November 4, 2014, Louisville, Kentucky.

39. Schaeffer, *How Now Shall We Live?*, 17.

40. Ibid., 478.

41. Ibid., 487.

42. Chuck Colson, "Foreword," in Frank R. Wolf and Anne Morse, *Prisoner of Conscience: One Man's Crusade for Global Human and Religious Rights* (Grand Rapids, MI: Zondervan, 2011), 10.

43. Interview with Frank Wolf, June 21, 2014, Washington, DC.

44. See Josh Good, "Colson as Prison Reformer," *The Weekly Standard*, April 27, 2012, accessible at http://www.weekly standard.com/blogs/colson-prison-reformer_642153.html.

45. Timothy George, "Be Not Afraid!," memorial service for Chuck Colson, May 16, 2012, accessible at http://www.bees ondivinity.com/fromthedean/posts/homily.

46. Chuck Colson, *The Sky Is Not Falling* (Brentwood, TN: Worthy, 2011), xiii.

47. Interview with Timothy George, August 7, 2014, Birmingham, Alabama.

48. Interview with Robert P. George, June 17, 2014, Washington, DC.

49. Laurie Goodstein, "Christian Leaders Unite on Political Issues," *New York Times*, November 20, 2009, accessible at www.nytimes.com/2009/11/20/us/politics/20alliance.html.

50. Interview with Robert P. George.

CHAPTER 7: TWILIGHT

1. Colson, *Dancing with Max*, 158.

2. Interview with Emily Colson, January 15, 2014, by phone.

3. Colson, *Dancing with Max*, 159.

4. Interview with Mark Dever, June 18, 2014, Washington, DC.

5. Interview with Gregory Thornbury, June 27, 2014, Louisville, Kentucky.
6. Interview with John Stonestreet, July 3, 2014, by phone.
7. Interview with David Carlson, June 17, 2014, Lansdowne, Virginia.
8. Interview with Alan Terwilliger, June 17, 2014, Lansdowne, Virginia.
9. Interview with Terwilliger.
10. Ibid.
11. Ibid.
12. Interview with Stan Gundry, November 18, 2013, Baltimore, Maryland.
13. Ibid.
14. Interview with Michael Cromartie, June 18, 2014, Washington, DC.
15. Charles Colson, *The Faith* (Grand Rapids, MI: Zondervan, 2008), 107.
16. Ibid., 109.
17. Colson, *The Faith*, 204.
18. Ibid., 206–7.
19. Ibid., 207.
20. Denny Burk, "Chuck Colson Calls Christians to Civil Disobedience Against U.S. Government," Denny Burk: A Commentary, Feb. 8, 2012, http://www.dennyburk.com/chuck -colson-calls-christians-to-civil-disobedience-against-u-s -government/.
21. http://breakingthespiralofsilence.com/.
22. Interview with Eric Metaxas, June 20, 2014, New York City.
23. Interview with Metaxas.
24. Interview with Terwilliger.
25. Interview with Carlson.
26. Michael Gerson, "Charles Colson Found Freedom in Prison," *Washington Post*, April 22, 2012, accessible at http://www .washingtonpost.com/opinions/finding-freedom-in-prison /2012/04/22/gIQANabcaT_story.html.

27. CBS News, "Woodward on Secret Service: Time to Fire Someone," April 23, 2012, accessible at http://www.cbsnews.com /news/woodward-on-secret-service-time-to-fire-someone.

28. http://chuckcolson.org/tributes.

29. Interview with Hayes Wicker, January 7, 2015, by phone.

30. Interview with Metaxas.

31. See Rodney Stark, *The Rise of Christianity: A Sociologist Reconsiders History* (Princeton, NJ: Princeton University Press, 1996).

CHAPTER 8: ONWARD

1. Roger Scruton, *Gentle Regrets* (London: Bloomsbury, 2006), 202.

2. Interview with Metaxas.

3. See Eric Metaxas, *Miracles: What They Are, Why They Happen, and How They Can Change Your Life* (New York: Dutton, 2014).

4. Jonathan Frantzen, *Freedom: A Novel* (New York: Strauss, Farrar, and Giroux, 2010), 559.

5. Wendell Berry, *Hannah Coulter: A Novel* (Berkeley: Counterpoint, 2005), 179.

6. Rod Dreher, *The Little Way of Ruthie Leming: A Southern Girl, a Small Town, and the Secret of a Good Life* (New York: Grand Central Publishing, 2013), 225.

7. See Jonathan Leeman, *Church Membership: How the World Knows Who Represents Jesus* (Carol Stream, IL: Crossway, 2012); Raymond C. Ortlund, Jr., *The Gospel: How the Church Portrays the Beauty of Christ* (Carol Stream, IL: Crossway, 2014).

8. Matthew Crawford, *Shop Class as Soulcraft: An Inquiry into the Value of Work* (New York: Penguin, 2009), 210.

9. Laurence Chandy and Geoffrey Gertz, "With Little Notice, Globalization Reduced Poverty," accessible at http://yaleglobal. yale.edu/content/little-notice-globalization-reduced-poverty.

10. See Richard John Neuhaus and Peter Berger, *Against the World for the World: The Hartford Appeal and the Future of American Religion* (New York: Seabury, 1976).

11. "The President Participates in a Ceremony for 2008 Recipients of the Presidential Citizens Medal," December 10, 2008, accessible at http://georgewbush-whitehouse.archives.gov/news /releases/2008/12/20081210–3.html.
12. Interview with Carlson.
13. Interview with Terwilliger.

ACKNOWLEDGMENTS

I am thankful to Erik Wolgemuth, who aided this project in every way. It was great to work with Webster Younce and, earlier, Joel Miller of Thomas Nelson, on a second book. My experience with Thomas Nelson has been exemplary on every level, and for that I am grateful.

To the litany of my interviewees, I owe a debt: Emily Colson, Eric Metaxas, John Stonestreet, Robert P. George, Timothy George, Frank Wolf, Hugh Hewitt, Michael Cromartie, Mark Dever, Erick Erickson, Alan Terwilliger, David Carlson, R. Albert Mohler, Jr., Gregory Thornbury, Andrew Walker, Eric Teetsel, Hayes Wicker, Matthew Schmitz, and John Michael LaRue. A special word of thanks to Steve Bradford and David Carlson of the Colson Center for Christian Worldview for their support. David and a number of other friends helped me greatly through their proofreading efforts. Any standing errors owe to me alone.

My colleagues at Southern Seminary and Boyce College encouraged me. Oren Martin listened to more updates about Colson than he likely ever thought possible. Denny Burk encouraged me to write this book. The generous leadership of R. Albert Mohler, Jr., Randy Stinson, and Dan DeWitt make it possible for faculty members to devote serious amounts of time to worthy projects. This is a rare gift, but not an unappreciated one.

I am blessed with an array of faithful friends. Andrew Walker sharpened me through a number of stimulating conversations. Gabe Molnar talked Colsonian strategy with me on numerous occasions. Grant Castleberry of the Council on Biblical Manhood and Womanhood prayed for me regularly. Eric Teetsel took a day to drive me all over Washington, DC. Brothers-at-arms Denny Burk, Jim Hamilton, and Ben Domenech spurred me on to write this book.

My family, both the Strachan and Ware sides, were a great help to me. My deepest thanks goes to my wife, Bethany, who is a tremendous help and encouragement to me. Without her support, I could not have written this book. "He who finds an excellent wife . . ." My children make me laugh, update me on the latest UPS deliveries, and write melting "I love you Daddy" cards that remind me why we enter public-square debate at all.

Finally, I acknowledge a debt to Eric Metaxas. Eric has written a very gracious foreword to this book, but even had he not, my study of Colson's public-square witness would seem incomplete without this acknowledgment. No one can or should be the next Chuck Colson. But it seems clear to me and many others that Eric has inherited Colson's mantle. He is a winsome yet convictional apologist for the Christian faith. The Lord has given him an unusually large platform. Like Colson, his mentor and friend, Eric uses it for God's glory, not his own. This book is itself a small approximation of the kind of work Eric has done in *Miracles*, *Bonhoeffer*, and other projects.

I never got to meet Chuck Colson. I wish I had. All my research has shown me very clearly that he lent great strength to those around him. He faced tremendous opposition, but he never stopped preaching the truth and reaching out to unbelievers with a smile on his face. In similar fashion, I derive great encouragement and courage from Eric, and I dedicate this book to him.

ABOUT THE AUTHOR

Owen Strachan is assistant professor of Christian theology and church history at the Southern Baptist Theological Seminary and Boyce College. He is the president of the Council on Biblical Manhood and Womanhood and the director of the Carl F. H. Henry Institute for Evangelical Engagement at SBTS. A graduate of Bowdoin College, he has authored seven books and written for outlets like *The Atlantic, National Review,* and *First Things.*